MW00720937

Break Up
Make Up
or
Shake Up

Redefining Relationships
in Retirement, Isolation & Crisis

Cathalynn Labonté-Smith

Manor House

Library and Archives Canada Cataloguing in Publication

Title: Break up, make up, or shake up : defining relationships in retirement, isolation & crisis / Cathalynn Labonté-Smith

Names: Labonté-Smith, Cathalynn, author.

Identifiers: Canadiana 20200363530 |

ISBN 9781988058610 (hardcover) |

ISBN 9781988058603 (softcover)

Subjects: LCSH: Man-woman relationships. | LCSH: Separation (Psychology) | LCSH: Rejection
(Psychology) | LCSH: Divorce—Psychological aspects. |
LCSH: Interpersonal relations. | LCSH: Dating (Social customs)
Classification: LCC HQ801 .L26 2020 | DDC 306.89-dc23ISBN

Publication Date: November 2020

Cover design: Michael Davie /Image: Ollyy / Shutterstock

Disclaimer: This book is not a substitute for professional help. For professional legal, financial, counselling, medical or other advice pertaining to your specific case, please refer to a lawyer, financial expert, counsellor, medical professional or other suitable professional. Names, locations and other identifying details contained in this book have been changed or deleted to conceal the identities of the individuals.

Funded by the Government of Canada | Canadä

To my husband for his blessing to tell our story and to my Chihuahuas for keeping my lap warm and face washed.

To all the courageous collaborators, who generously shared their stories and time to make this book have depth and humanity.

To the doctors, caregivers, first responders and leaders who kept us as safe as possible during the time of the COVID-19 pandemic.

- Cathalynn Labonté-Smith

Acknowledgements

Thank you to Vanessa Park, Family Law Attorney in Vancouver and my legal angel for her expertise, astute legal editing, enthusiasm, and patience in walking me through the staggering amount of details of divorce and family law.

Thanks to Dr. Tim Clark for his expertise in counselling couples in crisis.

A million thanks to the Gibsons Writers' Group for their encouragement and wisdom: Rosa Reid, Elizabeth Rains and Elspeth Richmond who provided much needed support.

Thanks to my first readers Heather Halverson, Michelle Woods, and Nyree Roy, who kept me going forward.

To my editor, Sue Chambers, for her keen eye, advice and resources.

To Christopher Powell for his candor and insight into financial matters.

To Jeff Hortobagyi for his careful thoughtful editing, and to Michael Davie and Manor House for Foreword, cover design-layout and publishing my book.

About the Author

Cathalynn Cindy Labonté-Smith grew up in Southwestern Alberta. She moved to Vancouver, BC, to complete her Bachelor of Fine Arts in Creative Writing at the University of British Columbia (UBC).

After graduation, she worked as a freelance journalist until present. She then became a technical writer in wireless communication and other high-tech industries. She went to UBC to complete a Bachelor of Education (Secondary) and taught English, Journalism, and other subjects at Vancouver high. As well, she has a Level I National Coach Certificate in Dragon Boating and Life Coach training.

She currently lives in Gibsons and North Vancouver, BC. She enjoys flying small planes as well as writing nonfiction, fibre arts and other crafts, playing with her chihuahuas, hanging out with her friends in coffee shops, and visiting family.

You can read her blogs at: www.wrtecup.wordpress.com and www.breakupmakeupshakeup.wordpress.com, where full links to resources and other bonus companion materials are available.

Break Up, Make Up or Shake Up / Cathalynn Labonté-Smith

Table of Contents:

Foreword: The Advice You're Seeking...

Are you in a difficult, unfulfilling relationship and you don't know where to go from here?

You have three basic choices, outlined in good detail in Cathalynn Labonté-Smith's helpful and insightful new book *Break Up, Make Up or Shake Up*.

If your best choice is to break up, this book contains a wealth of information on all of the legalities, options and approaches available – in Canada, the US, the UK, Australia and New Zealand – along with planning advice, examination of needed documents and insightful case histories, tips on dealing with violence, and much more.

Or, are you ready to reconcile and make up? If so, you'll also find some great advice on how to best go about making up and restoring your relationship with work by both parties, including better communication and the steps you'll both need to take for successful results.

Perhaps, what you really need is a good shake up - a redefining of your relationship under new terms and conditions that are a departure from the past – terms that are fair and considerate to you both via mutual agreement.

You'll find terrific advice, illustrative true-life stories, key information, clear-cut approaches – and a good deal more - including tips on coping with all of this during a pandemic! It's timely advice at any time and it's all here in the pages of this well-written, remarkably informative book. This is your road map to whichever journey you choose – a highly recommended, informative must-read!

- **Michael B. Davie**, author, *Great Advice*

Break Up, Make Up or Shake Up / Cathalynn Labonté-Smith

Introduction: My journey to another life…

All happy families are alike; each unhappy family is unhappy in its own way.
- Leo Tolstoy, *Anna Karenina*

"You're taking an awful lot this time." My heart pounded, as if my husband was an armed security guard at the bank and I had a suitcase full of cold hard cash. I was about to walk out on my husband of 32 years, and I didn't want him to know until I was at my hide-away.

In the bottom of my purse, was a fat brown envelope full of copies of our personal documents, plus our original marriage certificate, my passport and a wad of American cash. I was a thief, stealing the contents of our file cabinet and lockbox. I was just a few steps away from my getaway car. Well, it was a Prius, nevertheless it had four wheels and two motors.

My grey spinner suitcase was packed by the front door, as I prepared to make my way by ferry to our condo in the city. However, this trip I also had a box of books, baskets of craft items, a spare sewing machine and some treasured personal items too. The Chihuahuas sniffed and scratched among my belongings when "Ace" (not his real name) came down the stairs, folded his arms and stood by the pile.

"Yep," I said, offering no explanation. He was like airport security — a TSA agent with x-ray eyes scrutinizing me as I loaded the hybrid car with my belongings. The little dogs trotted in and out of the house begging to go with me.

"How long are you going for this time?" he asked.

"I'm not sure," I said and gave him a quick kiss before I closed the hatch. I picked up each tiny dog and hugged them, trying not to reveal too much of my heartache in front of him.

I hopped into my escape car and backed down the curved driveway, saying a mental goodbye to my dream home, the house that we got when it was only two years-old, with its bay window overlooking the ocean, prairie style lines anchored with cedar posts on a half-acre on the Sunshine Coast of BC. A wilderness home still frequented by deer, bears and cougars, peered at by eagles by day and owls by night, and visited by humming-birds under the cloud of evergreen clematis blossoms that I'd planted as soon as we moved in.

As I drove down the hill in the Prius, I saw the gleaming white ferry approach the dock below. I was nervous as I waited in the parking lot for an hour to board, because he could still come after me. It was time to drive up the iron ramp. I could take a breath again.

I sat in my car on the ferry watching the waves and seagulls play in the wind both stunned and excited. *How could this have happened to us?* When he retired at 56 years-old, I expected adventure, travel and deeper intimacy. However, what I got was a ghost who haunted the den upstairs. I sat at the bottom of the steps and mourned the loss of my soulmate. Alive, but dead to me.

Imagine if you were in my place, we lived together two years before we got married and had just celebrated our 30th anniversary that January. I looked forward to the best time of our lives to begin. However, he closed the door on his den and didn't come out except to eat and sleep for about a year, while I pined and mourned at the bottom of the steps for the loss of my soulmate.

After forty minutes the ship pulled into the dock, (so it wasn't an epic sea voyage) and I drove into my new life. I stopped in at a bookstore to find guidance in the self-help section. There were only a few books on divorce and zero for people entering singlehood in their 50s. There were no books online either that contained all I needed to know. The more research I did, the more I realized I needed to write this book.

I'm not a relationship guru, or a lawyer, or financial advisor, but I worked extra hard to give you all that I discovered in working my way through not only my split, but also what others went through and what the processes were in other countries.

Those people who have walked in your shoes once before and sometimes more than once, they got you. Myself, and all the people I interviewed are here walking beside you. The professionals that give solid advice, they got you too. You may end up breaking up with your partner, or you may end up rekindling your love. Whatever the outcome may be, remember you are a strong person to have got this far.

That was the start of my plan to separate. I lived full-time on the Sunshine Coast before we got a place in the city. I reached out to friends to see if they knew of a place I could stay.

A couple who lived near my old neighbourhood were going away on a trip in January. They would let me stay at their place for several weeks. I kept that information to myself until Christmas was over. I didn't want to ruin our last Christmas together.

 I'd been warned by friends, who had been through this milestone, when I announced that Ace was retiring to expect a tumultuous few years. I thought, that's them, but my Ace is such an easy-going guy and we have a plan. . .we're different.

We were going to travel, read and blog, maybe, he would pick up a contract in one of those places-you-want-to-go-to-before-you-die. Ace is only 56 years-old—he's going to be different.

Then a year later, there I was looking desperately through the Self-Help section at the bookstore, finding no books for Canadians entering singlehood in their grey years. There were no books online either for this Canuck gal, or at least if there were they were doing a great job of hiding them.

Not that I'm actually silver or grey-haired, in my early 50s I have just a tiny bit of grey starting to show here and there, but those suckers are easily covered up with trips to the salon. Ace keeps his hair shaved so he doesn't really count as a silver fox either.

I enjoyed my time apart during this trial separation. Afterwards, I pushed to purchase a wee condo in the city. I found myself spending more and more time there connecting with old friends and making new friendships; however, Ace continued to nest in the country.

After a few months, I found myself here in my car with a trunk full of my most critical possessions on the ferry deck.

Until this happened to me and Ace, I didn't know that the largest growing sector of divorces fit our profile: long-married couples over 50, who are retired. Statistics Canada reported, in 2011, that 328,920 Canadians aged 60-64 divorced and more women were initiating divorces, representing 16% of that population (Manisha Krishhnan, 2012).

Across the border the number of silver splitters are increasing rapidly as well, "Seniors age 50 to 64 are divorcing at four times higher than the national average... using US Census Bureau data. In the last 10 years, divorce among seniors has increased 50 per cent," (Joe Piedimonte, 2016).

I felt so alone until I did copious research and discovered that *grey divorce* or *silver separation*, so-called for the colour of mature hair, is a world-wide trend (Wendy Dennis, 2016). Despite these ageist terms, as many of us colour our hair (men too) and many people don't go completely grey, I felt less alone, especially, when I discovered most partners who left were women, at least in heterosexual couples. There's not a lot of information on same-sex couples, because same-sex marriages don't have a lot of history internationally — yet.

15

Retirement was the trigger for why I left Ace, as it is for many women of my vintage. For over 30 years Ace was rarely home during weekday work hours, plus he was frequently on business trips. Suddenly, he was home 24/7, but ironically unavailable to me which magnified our marital issues.

The common factor that initiates many a silver separation and grey divorce is the retirement of the male partner. As Dr. Tim Clark, a Registered Psychologist in North Vancouver, explains, "The economic reasons for staying together are disappearing. Women are redefining marriage as they aren't dependent on men."

In the US, the rate of grey divorce is increasing rapidly:
From 1990 to 2008, the divorce rate among men 65 and older doubled from 5 to 10 percent. Among women 65 and older, it tripled from 4 to 12 percent. In 2010. . .among baby boomers from age 50 to 64. . .divorce rate is four times higher than the 65-plus age group. . .Today one in four people in this age group are getting divorced in this age group. . .and it could increase another 25 percent in the next 20 years. (J. Piedimonte, 2016).

The reasons for mature women world-wide pulling the ripcord on their marriages include:

- They have good paying jobs that allow financial independence;

- They are knowledgeable about their entitlement to spousal support and their share of their partner's pension;

- They have pensions, savings and investments of their own.

Dr. Clark likens marriage to a business partnership, in that a couple unites in the business of raising children, making a home and building careers.

When the children leave home couples need to, "Rewrite the deal." (For some couples, the children leaving the home is metaphorical, as millennials may live at home long past their expected launch date, such as the milestones of graduating from high-school and university) He advises they need a joint discussion or they will "sink and drown". (Interview, June 22, 2017).

I'd seen my parents go through an adjustment period when they retired and moved to a new town, but their marriage survived so what was their secret?

My parents were even younger than we were when they married. I was born when my mother was barely 20 years-old and now they've been together more than 53 years. They were business partners through most of their working lives, first running an antique and second-hand store together, Trader Vic's, then a dog kennel, Cecile's Kennels.

Essentially, spending 24/7 together through two businesses, plus the business of raising two daughters together. Now that they're retired they dance together, love to wear matching outfits down to the same red sneakers, play a Rummy tile game a couple times a day, do projects around the house and are adorable.

Although, they would call it "discussing" or "communicating" not bickering, to a third-party it sounds rather like a perpetual argument, but to them it's just part of how they've gotten along for more than half a century.

There are general books on splitting up for the so-called "starter marriage", but there were no books for a silver splitter with my needs, so I decided to write one.

After all, I started my journalism career when I was still in high-school, as a reporter and photographer for the local paper as part of a career program. I had a column about the hilarities of campus life at the *University of Lethbridge* from the age of seventeen.

I made a living as a freelancer throughout the 90s when I found a niche market writing about the human-computer interface.

I've continued to write articles about whatever I was interested in until the present.

I also spent over fifteen years as a technical writer for high tech companies writing about everything from banking, to medical imaging systems to wireless communication systems.

I can do this, I thought, I can gather all the information I need to get through this process in one place not only for myself, but also for other people going through the same thing.

While some families run with wolves or scissors, our family runs with pens.

My paternal great-grandmother was a journalist—writing a local newspaper in her small town. My grandmother wrote prolific legendary letters.

My dad wrote a side-splitting book, called *Second-hand First-hand* (unpublished), about the years he ran his antique/second-hand store, plus he's authored countless country songs.

I grew up reading my late uncle's newsletter, *The Redneck News* — seriously, that was the title. Another uncle wrote sermons for his parish and reams of poetry. I have a cousin who's won awards for his plays. Needless to say, the emails we write to each other are epic.

I used my lifetime of experience as a journalist, interviewer, writer, researcher and teacher to draft this book within a month. My goal is to walk beside my readers through this process of separating in the most painless way possible.

I thought that if it took me every waking hour in that concentrated, but still significant amount of time to pull that information together, the average person going through this highly emotional and confusing experience, who may have aging parents and/or children to care for on top of the separation, or wouldn't have the time, energy or background to do this deeper inquiry for themselves.

We, older folk, need different texts than younger people, because when you're over 50 there are critical differences when uncoupling, as follows.

We don't have the number of years left that younger couples do to rebuild finances, start new relationships, climb back up the property ladder. Two-thirds of our lives may be behind us.

Given all the strong medications I need to take for my arthritis and the effect they have on my organs, probably less than one-third of my life is ahead of me.

We also have extra people to care for, like grandchildren, step-children and aging parents. For example, I'm fortunate that Ace continues to help with the care of my parents, mainly in the form of logistics and technical support.

In the early stages of separation, he lives in our marital home on the Coast of BC and I live in a condo in North Vancouver.

My family, including my parents, who are in their early 70s, live two ferry trips away from me, a journey that takes at least five hours one way to complete.

Ace lives between me and my family at one ferry trip between myself and my family. He's extremely gracious and helps with my parents' medical trips to the Vancouver area, letting them stay over at our marital home and/or dropping them at the ferry terminal for me to pick up.

Just because we may be breaking up doesn't mean we have to be unkind to each other or each other's family, in fact, things are quite amicable. I can only hope that it continues to be so.

Ace and I weren't lucky enough to have children, so we don't have the complexity of children (minor, adult or special needs), grandchildren to navigate. We do have two adorable chihuahuas we rescued from Mexico; however, so we do what's best for the wee doggies.

The chis love being at the country home romping around the half-acre of the Chihuahua-proofed fenced yard. They spend the sunny days lounging in the sun and barking at anything that moves, including birds, squirrels, deer, bears, falling leaves, pine cones and other life-threatening objects.

Together, we have many niblings (the group noun of nieces and nephews). I reckon, it will be painful for some and some will carry on as if it'd never happened. All of them are young adults now, except for one and that makes it easier.

I had an uncle who has passed away, that married, divorced and remarried the same aunt several times.

However, my uncle lived many ferries away from us and the divorces never had any impact on me. I know it was difficult for my cousins, to be go back and forth between the parents during their feuds, but what aunts and uncles got up to made no difference to me.

They lived apart in different areas of the province from each other, getting together just long enough to "honeymoon," as my aunt put it.

The only way I could relate to my cousins' experience is one day my parents sat me and my sibling down and asked us if we had to choose, not that we were making an actual choice, just in theory, if we had to choose which parent would we live with if Mommy and Daddy split up.

We both chose a different parent which made us bawl. I tried to convince my younger sister to stay together with me with the parent I'd chosen, but she wanted to stay with her chosen parent which made us cling to each other and cry even more.

Our parents started to choke up too and that was the end of the discussion. When I was an adult, my mother admitted that they really were contemplating a split but seeing our reaction made them decide to work things out.

My parents have been married for 53 years and Ace's over 55 years, so with over 108 years of marital bliss as role models before us, what is wrong with us?

My parents idolize Ace to the point when he's around, I'm Ace's wife rather than their daughter.

I waited as long as possible before telling them we were separated. I only told them because Ace's name is all over their legal documents — they truly consider them their son not just a son-in-law. I think if they had a choice, they would pick him over me to keep, but unfortunately for them I am their genetic material and as my Dad pointed out recently in an email to me — I can't divorce my dad. I begged them not to put his names on their documents, in case he traded me in for a peppier younger model, but they had their reasons.

My dad said to tell Ace, "He's my best and only buddy. I'm going to keep being his friend."

In fact, when Dad saw a picture of me with a male friend of mine from grade school sitting together posted on social media, he sent me a scathing email about my disrespectful behaviour.

Not that it was any of his business, but I explained to Dad that we were sitting near my friend's lovely wife who wasn't in the frame.

I agreed with him that Ace was a great catch and hoped he found a wonderful woman to share his life with, if we couldn't work things out. Dad calmed down and apologized.

About this Book

The purpose of this book is to walk you through the process of breaking up or making up or shaking up – altering your relationship - starting from the time you realize you want to leave your partner, or your partner leaves you, and going full circle to when you start your new life either with or without your partner.

 You may find it useful to refer back again to this book when you start a new relationship as well.

Scope of this Book

The scope of this book covers how to proceed with a separation, divorce, and suggests strategies on how to stay together.

The separation and divorce guidelines for the following countries are included:

- Canada
- United States
- United Kingdom
- Australia
- New Zealand

When to Use this Book

The timeline to use the book is ideally before you leave your partner, or if you suspect your partner is going to leave you, and within that first year of separation when there are so many changes that happen to your day-to-day life.

Everyone breaks up from a committed relationship at their own pace. You may find you need a long time to get up the courage to leave. You may leave and then reconcile with your partner. Your partner may leave you and return multiple times, before breaking away forever. This book will take you through the process of breaking up wherever you happen to be at.

What is in This Book:

This book reflects not only my journey, but also the wisdom of those who shared their stories and the advice of the professionals I interviewed.

At the beginning of a breakup I wanted to know critical questions from them, such as:

- How did I get here? Why am I going through a separation now after over three decades?

- Do I even need a lawyer? How could I do this as painlessly as possible for both of us?

- How do I protect myself?

- What should I expect during and after the uncoupling process?

- What terminology do I need to know?

- How much is this going to cost?

- How long does a divorce take?

- What professionals should I see?

- What resources are available?

- Am I doing the right thing?

- What do I do now?

- How do I reconcile?

For readers breaking up in the aftermath of the pandemic there are answers to the question, *How is the COVID-19 pandemic going to affect this process?*

As you read the stories throughout the book, you'll see other people who went through multiple traumas, including physical, verbal and emotional abuse, the death of a child or of a soulmate.

The people I interviewed, who were in an abusive relationship are happier for leaving.

In fact, they wish they'd left their partner years before. Leaving an abusive relationship was non-negotiable. They're on the healing path to finding peace or they have already found it with someone new or on their own.

***

Happy couples don't get divorced. Unhappy couples need this book.

***

My interviewees shared something sacred and often their story was a secret they never shared with anyone else before. They found telling their tale to be a salve on their wounds.

I believe the stories from these elders and survivors carry healing powers.

As one of these brave contributors, "Tara," said: "We all have our stories to tell and eventually our journeys come to end, and we move on. I think our stories will give people encouragement and mostly let them know they're not alone."

Exercises

The optional exercises throughout this book can assist you in gathering information that may prove helpful in the offices of your counselor or lawyer, or in conversations with your partner. On a separate piece of paper, jot down your responses to the following exercise:

Exercise 1. Reasons for breakup

Couples will have two stories of why they split up, or three if they're a thruple; however, the main two reasons appear to be abuse and cheating. More reasons are described in Krishnan's article *For Better or Divorce*.

You know the reasons why you are leaving, but here's a recap of the main reasons: Abuse; Affair; Boredom;

Disappointment; Fed up; Finances; Health issues; Interests; Moving; Personal growth or lack thereof ; Power shift; Priorities ; Retired Partner Syndrome (RPS); Not enough space (as we discovered during the Covid-19 pandemic).

Reflect and write about why you're breaking up with your partner. This can be helpful later when you seek legal or counselling help, as they'll want to know the core problems. On a separate piece of paper or on a computer jot down answers to: What will divorce look like to you? What timeframe would you expect your divorce to take?

Why You Need This Book

What brought you to this book? Did you come home one day to a sticky note on the fridge that said your partner never wants to see you again? Or after years of drifting apart, that fine thread binding you together stretched farther and farther apart until it broke?

Are you wondering what your next steps are?

You will find within this book what to do when your partnership breaks down, whether you are legally married or living together in a common-law marriage, or domestic partnership.

Anyone who is newly single, in a relationship but struggling, married and going through a separation or divorce, or who is Di-Curious (a term invented by Barry Gold within the book *Gray Divorce Stories: The Truth About Getting Divorced Over 50 From Men and Women Who've Done it*), will benefit from reading this book.

You'll also find answers to questions about how you can go forward with a separation during the time of the COVID-19 pandemic. Diana Isaac, a partner at the family law firm Shulman & Partners LLP in Toronto, told CBC she's seen a 40% increase in calls from couples seeking to end their marriages since the pandemic began.

Ideally, this book can be shared by both partners involved in the split. Also, anyone affected by the split, such as extended family members and adult children or adult grandchildren, may gain insight into what the divorcing couple is going through by reading this book.

Also, professionals who provide services to people going through divorce and separation, such as real estate agents, lawyers and financial advisors will benefit from reading this book and giving a copy to their clients.

A Pandemic Looking-glass into Retired Life Together

My situation was difficult enough but at least I had the option to physically leave in 2016.

However, let's zoom ahead four years and it's now May 2020 during the full force of the COVID-19 pandemic. You've been confined with your partner for 24/7 for months and it could still be additional months or even an entire year before anything close to normal life resumes.

After this extended period of togetherness, perhaps in a small apartment where you're both working from home (WFH), you discover that they drive you nuts. Did you think, *Help! I'm stuck with my spouse and I feel suffocated. I see what our future together as an old retired married couple will be like and I want out of this now?*

What if you couldn't physically leave whilst in self-quarantine? As a friend said to me recently, "And that space lack is more than just physical. I find it to be psychological, emotional, everything."

"You know this is a glimpse into what retirement is going to look like for you two ten years from now, if you can't sort out your issues now," I said.

When Wuhan, China lifted restrictions after quarantine from the COVID-19 virus, divorce rates soared according to an article by Meaghan Wray, *China's divorce rates rise as couples emerge from coronavirus quarantine.*

Not only because of the financial stress and strain that the loss of one or both of their jobs brought, but also because after spending so much time with their partners couples got a glimpse into what their future would be like when they retired together.

"If your marriage isn't in a great place, it might be you're pouring gasoline on a fire by being around each other 24/7," said divorce attorney Jason Hopper," in an article by Kelly Hesseldal. Hopper is a California lawyer, who received 500 more calls a week about divorce than before the pandemic; double his usual number of divorce queries.

Many couples didn't like what that future looked like behind those non-medical masks. Without outside jobs, activities, family and friends to spend time away from each other their problems were magnified.

Suddenly, couples were plunged into the same mode as retired couples, who were ill-prepared for retirement.

Improperly Prepared for Retirement

Being ill-prepared for retirement can mean the following work wasn't done ahead of time:

- You don't have the funds to maintain the lifestyle you had prior to retirement. Hopefully, you won't have to totally rely on the government pensions at 65.

- You haven't cultivated interests outside of work, so you or your spouse don't know what to do with yourselves with all the free time you now have.

- You haven't spent time planning what you will do together once you retire, or you're at odds at how to spend your retirement and what mutual goals you want to set.

- You move to a home in a new community, down-sized, or went off the grid, and one or both of you are regretting it. You lost your social connections or feel like you're living on top of each other.

- You expect your physical health to remain the same. For example, you bought a dream home on the waterfront with four flights of stairs and your knees gave out in the first year. Or, you open a B&B for retirement income and your back develops problems.

- You are forced to retire, so you are resentful and angry.

- You believed you could work forever, so you never had a retirement plan.

Looking at the list of possible triggers for divorce, it's difficult to avoid all the pitfalls. My partner and I fell victim to two of them. We didn't create a vision together and we moved to a place where I struggled to fit in and missed my social connections.

Grey Wave of Divorce

In the US, the number of silver splitters is increasing rapidly as well. In Joe Piedimonte's book, *When Gray Divorce Strikes,* he says, "Seniors aged 50 to 64 are divorcing at a rate four times higher than the national average. Divorce among seniors has increased 50%."

The international trend of grey divorce is found not only Canada, but also in the US, where the the the number of silver splitters is increasing rapidly as well. In Joe Piedimonte's book, *When Gray Divorce Strikes,* he says, "Seniors aged 50 to 64 are divorcing at a rate four times higher than the national average. Divorce among seniors has increased 50%."

The same trend is found across the pond in the UK for silver splicers, where the UK Office of Statistics found that in the 65 and older group men are divorcing 23% more frequently and women by 38%.

Australians married for 20 years or more are divorcing 27% more often than in the past, according to the Australian Government. Statistics New Zealand reported in 2015 that 11.7% of divorces were between couples married for more than 30 years.

I felt less alone, especially when I discovered that most of the partners who left were the women.

***

How is grey divorce different? For couples over 50, there are critical differences when uncoupling, as follows:

- We don't have the number of years left that younger couples do to rebuild finances, start new relationships, and climb back up the property ladder with two-thirds of our lives behind us.

- We have many who depend on us, such as grandchildren, adult children, step-children, aging parents and beloved pets in the picture. Ace and I weren't lucky enough to have children, so we don't have the complexity of children (minor, adult, or special needs) and grandchildren to navigate.

- We may be preparing to retire or are already retired, so pensions and savings are all we have left to live on. Will it be enough? Will we have to go back to work? Will we have to sell our home?

- Fear of being alone and sick. We may have health issues and/or self-esteem issues making it terrifying to leave our long-term partner. With good friends, family, and resilience we can manage. After all, there were times that I had to rely on others when Ace travelled for business.

- We may think that people our age just don't get divorced — **myth.** We're living longer, and the partner that suited us in our youth and mid-life might not suit us in our remaining years.

The common factor that initiates many silver separations and grey divorces is the retirement of the male partner. As Dr. Tim Clark, a Registered Psychologist in North Vancouver, explains, "The economic reasons for staying together are disappearing. Women are redefining marriage as they aren't dependent on men."

Reasons why mature women all over the world are no longer dependent on men and are pulling the ripcord on their marriages include:

- They have well-paying jobs that allow financial independence.

- They are knowledgeable about their entitlement to spousal support and their share of their partner's pension.

- They have pensions, savings and investments of their own.

Dr. Clark likens marriage to a business partnership in that a couple unites in the business of raising children, making a home, and building careers. When the children leave home it's an important time for couples to "rewrite the deal." (For some couples, the children leaving the home is metaphorical as millennials may live at home long past their expected launch date, such as the milestones of graduating from high school and university).

He advises couples to have a discussion between themselves when they become empty nesters about how they will now organize the household. For example, if one spouse did all the cooking and cleaning for the family, maybe it's time to share household tasks equally.

FAQ - How Do I Keep My Partner from Knowing What I've Looked at on My Browser?

To keep what you do on the Internet private and anonymous, there are different levels of security to take depending on how tech savvy the person you don't want to know what you are doing is. This includes keeping your browsing history private or sending emails that can't be traced back to you.

Keeping your browser history private by deleting it after you're finished might work, but there are a number of security breaches that can happen:

1. You may forget to delete it one time.

2. Most browsers synchonize this to all your devices, like your tablet, laptop and cell phone, so it may still remain on one of them.

3. The information is used for other purposes like auto-suggest, so Google may suggest something based on a previous search that you don't want seen.

4. Ads could pop up based on your searches, for example, for divorce attorneys.

The newer and better way is to use your browser's Incognito mode to do your private browsing.

Every browser has a different way of using Incognito mode, so use Google for instructions on how to use it with your browser. This is a good way to stay private, but:

1. A person could still shoulder surf to see what you're doing.

2. Companies like Google, Microsoft and your Internet Service Provider (ISP) have a record of your sessions and can be subpoenaed for that information.

3. It doesn't make applications you use more private, like email or social media.

For a higher level of privacy, follow these guidelines:

1. Use a computer that isn't affiliated with you in any way, like at a library or Internet cafe.

2. Don't login to any of your usual email or social media apps, because as soon as you login everything else you do can be traced.

3. At a safe computer create a new secret email and/or social media accounts and never login to them from your home or work computers.

4. Ensure there is no way to trace them back to yourself by not using any personal information.

A good book on keeping yourself safe online is *The Art of Invisibility* by Kevin Mitnick.

FAQ – What is a Separation
Separation occurs when a couple, either married or common-law, moves apart from each other.

FAQ - What is a Legal Separation
A legal separation is applied for through the courts and is just like a divorce, except that the couple is still married and unable to remarry.

CHAPTER 1: These Boots Were Made for Walking

All happy families are alike; each unhappy family is unhappy in its own way.
- Leo Tolstoy, *Anna Karenina*

My own love story is a simple one. Girl moves into the top floor of a house. Girl meets boy living in the basement.

Two weeks later they fall in love and are together for over thirty years. Boy retires, driving the girl crazy. Girl zips up her black sparkly boots and wants a divorce one January some 35 years later (January is the busiest month for divorce lawyers after all that seasonal togetherness).

I moved to Vancouver in 1983 to finish my undergraduate degree at the University of British Columbia (UBC) in the Creative Writing program. I checked the campus housing board and found a notice for a room in a house.

As I got to the house, I noted that it was as neglected as it was cheap. A guy answered the door — tall, thin, with long blonde hair that hung in his eyes. He flicked his hair back to reveal clear blue eyes behind silver-framed glasses and a shy smile.

He led me up the creaky splintered stairs to the room. He wore a slumped Cowichan sweater and jeans and radiated a golden light. Wait, what? A golden aura? The room was spacious, the window was permanently stuck open at the top, and there was a lumpy mattress on the floor.

"How much is the damage deposit?" I asked.

"There's no damage deposit," the lady I was replacing chimed in, "It's damaged enough." "I'll take it," I said. I wouldn't say I took the room with the permanent draft in the house with just one bathroom shared between eleven people and two scruffy dogs that left the tub fur-lined, just to be around the tall young man with the golden glow. However, I thought if someone as nice and normal as him could live there then I'd be okay.

We walked the two massive dogs. Zachary, a blue Malamute cross, left behind by the couple whose room I rented and Warrick, a red Irish Wolfhound. I told him all about my woeful past relationships. I vowed to spend my life single, because it was best for my writing career.

"You never know, the next one might be the right one," he said. It was then that I knew he was interested in me. One Saturday we headed to Stanley Park and strolled along the seawall. I almost reached out to hold his hand.

He took me to dinner. We went back to our house. I noticed my shoulders were sore, probably from hunching over the typewriter for my writing assignments. I asked him for a neck rub, which advanced to a back rub on the shapeless dusty couch that had probably been sourced from an alley. We ended up in his single bed in the basement. To think we were just housemates two weeks ago.

After another month of sharing one bathroom with nearly a dozen roomies we decided to get a place together. After marrying in 1987, starting our own company and saving every dollar we could, we got our first home in a sunny suburb. I had a couple of emergency surgeries that meant we'd never have children, so the focus of our lives became different than other couples.

We lived there for ten sun-drenched, beach-side years until we could afford a place in Vancouver.

For fifteen years we enjoyed the Vancouver community we were in. But Ace felt it was time to leave his position at a software company. We moved into our secondary home on the Sunshine Coast that we bought as part of our transition to early retirement plan.

I was excited that we'd at last be together forever. Should we start with a trip across Canada in a travel trailer? Take a world cruise? The possibilities were so tantalizing.

The reality was that our marriage began to dissolve, as I spent over a year lonely, sad and miserable. He may as well still have been working and on business trips for all I saw him.

I thought we had a plan, where we would travel, do more things together, spend more time with family, or was it just me talking about those things?

***

It's all about balance of time spent apart and together — too much of either is unhealthy.

***

It's not that I wanted to spend all our time together, but some time together during the day would have gone a long way to prevent our separation.

A typical day together might look something like this:

Cat's Ideal Day with Ace

8:00 am - Sleep in. No need to leap out of bed anymore.

8:30 am - Walk the dogs.

9:00 am - 11 am - Go for coffee and write.

Noon - 1 pm - Back at home for lunch.

1 - 2:30 pm - Do individual or joint projects and/or chores.

2:30 pm - Walk the dogs.

3 - 3:30 pm - Teatime.

3:30 pm - 6:00 pm - Back to individual/joint projects/chores. If it's nice out, lay on a blanket together outside and read and/or nap. Or, sit out on the patio for happy hour.

6:00 pm - 7:00 pm - Watch the news and have a snack.

7 - 8:30 pm - TV, and/or projects/chores.

8:30 pm - Walk the dogs.

9:00 pm - 10:00 pm - Wind down for bed. Read. Play with the dogs.

Exercise 2. Your own Ideal Day Together
If you want an ideal day together with your partner, what would it look like? Make it as detailed as possible,

including where you'd want to be, what you'd want to eat, what activities you'd like to do morning, noon and night. You may want to present this to your partner and see what their ideal day would look like.

Ace and I had difficult but productive conversations. He became more open to discussing our problems.

My work life as a high-school teacher seemed drab in comparison to Ace's. He told me about his safaris in South Africa, or about watching the sunrise at the peak of Mount Kinabalu. I wasn't jealous of the grind that business travel can be—the strain of air travel, crossing multiple time zones and eating strange food.

Now that he was retired, Ace didn't want to go anywhere. The travel trailer sat in the driveway. But once I left Ace, I went on mini-vacays by myself, visiting friends, having fun and got a lot of writing done.

We didn't have gritty problems that some spouses endure, such as an abusive relationship, addictions or financial problems. He tried hard to fix us by working on a list I gave him. I didn't want to make a list, but it was hard for him to understand what I meant when I said the best thing anyone can do is to work on themselves.

Love's Light Went Out
Compared to the reasons people I interviewed split up, mine seemed petty, as there was no abuse, but the reasons are specific to the person and the relationship.

There was a moment when the steadfast feeling of being in love with Ace left me. It was as if there were an electric switch in the middle of my chest that flicked from "on" to "off." I wish I could turn it back on, as it would make life so much easier. I didn't think a couples' counsellor could bring that feeling back, but maybe I was wrong. If I had it to do over again, I would book us in to see a counsellor not only for their perspective, but also once I saw how many people were involved in the uncoupling process and the effort involved, we might have been better off putting our energy into making up rather than breaking up.

Pandemic Partners

It's been almost three years since I left Ace. It's March 2020 and Canada is shut down due to the COVID-19 pandemic. I was taking flying lessons out of the Bellingham Airport in Washington when the Canada-US border closed. I was nearly ready for my final check ride to get my private pilot certificate.

I switched to flying with my friend, Chris, from Pitt Meadows Airport for a while longer before the flight school shut down.

Our last flight was to Kamloops on March 18th. The next day, I put away my headset and other pilot gear in a closet. I hug the man standing in front of me with tears in my eyes and a lump in my throat.

"I wonder when this quarantine will be over and I can fly again," I said.

Ace held me tightly and said, "Not for a few months."

Spoiler alert: Ace and I reconciled our differences just a few months into our separation. Of all the people to be locked down with, I'm so glad I was with Ace. He's so easy-going and pleasant. The lockdown wasn't easy as was the case for everyone, but we felt fortunate that we had each other and our dogs for comfort.

***

I don't know what our lives in self-isolation would've been like, if we had split up when we hit that bump in the road three years ago. I can't imagine that it would've been better.

Getting through quarantine alone would've been even more difficult, than it was with someone as pleasant and reassuring as my Ace. It was scary sometimes, right? As I'm writing this it's still scary and it seems endless, even though I know we've got this, and it won't be forever.

If Ace and I had both been in new relationships, perhaps the kinks might not have been worked out yet. Statistically, second and subsequent marriages have less of a chance of succeeding as first marriages. Perhaps, proving that the first marriage is likely the best if we give it the time and attention it deserves.

So how did we mend our relationship that had such a huge communication chasm? Interviewing friends about their relationships, both current and past, while researching this book was extremely helpful. Also, Ace admitted that he retreated after his retirement. One day that love switch I talked about turned to the On position again. We have that harmonious long-lasting relationship again.

I still enjoy time in the city pursuing my writing interests and now having adventures flying small aircraft.

Ace enjoys his writing books, his HAM radio club, mountain biking, running, volunteering in the local Search and Rescue organization, teaching programming to kids, photography club and several computer programming clubs.

But we were able to craft ourselves a new relationship, that's more satisfying for both of us. Many couples do this with the help of a third-party, like a counsellor or even a good friend, but we were able to manage this on our own.

Moving Forward

When we first got back together, Ace and I set relationship goals, including:

- Make and support each other in becoming the best person we can be.

- Having more fun together.

- Going on more trips.

- Increasing our intimacy.

- Communicating more— starting with biweekly meetings.

While lying on a quilt watching clouds go by in the backyard, Ace told me about the latest relationship book he was reading as part of his goal to read one relationship book per month, *Making Marriage Simple, 10 Relationship-Saving Truths* by Harville Hendrix and Helen LaKelly Hunt. Ace felt the analogy of the "Turtle vs. the Hailstorm" was most relevant to us, how in every relationship there is a "turtle" who tends to withdraw and the "hailstorm" that tends to rain on the turtle. We discussed how to be less turtle and less hailstorm. Good meeting.

As you read the true stories in this book, I hope you find some that resonate with you and what they have to say helps you with your situation. You got this.

Exercise 3. Write what You Want from Your Partner
You don't need to share this with your partner; although it could be a turning point for your relationship if written with kindness and thoughtfulness. On a separate piece of paper or on your computer, write what you want from him or her.

***

FAQ - What is a No-Fault Divorce?

All divorces in Canada are "no-fault", meaning regardless of the behaviour of the parties, there is no blame laid on either that affects the division of assets and property. There are only three conditions for divorce, in Canada, as stated in Alison Sawyer's book, *British Columbia Do Your Own Divorce Kit:*

1. **If you are legally married, after one year of living separately, you or your partner, or both of you can file for an uncontested divorce.** You can file for divorce even if the other party doesn't want a divorce after a year. Or, you may decide to file for divorce at a later date or never. This is the most common reason and easiest path.

2. **Adultery.** Your spouse had sex with someone outside the marriage. If your spouse signs an affidavit admitting to the adultery, the divorce can be immediate; if your spouse won't sign the

affidavit, you have to prove the infidelity. This can be difficult to prove and not recommended as grounds.

3. **Cruelty.** Your spouse is inflicting mental and/or physical cruelty, and it's impossible and unsafe for you to live with them. This can be difficult to prove and isn't recommended as grounds.

Sawyer says that, "The *Divorce Act* allows for attempts at reconciliation . . . and [spouses] can reside together for a period (in total during the one-year period) of less than 90 days."

***

FAQ - Divorce During COVID-19 Pandemic Yes or No?

The short answer is "No," due to the courts being shut down, for example, in Canada and other countries, except for emergencies involving mostly criminal cases. The shutdown of the court system created a backlog of cases.

Lawyers offices are/were open to phone calls only. Enquiries regarding separation and divorce can/could still be made. Laurie H. Pawlitza's article, *Can I Get Divorced During the COVID-19 Pandemic and Other Burning Law Questions.* mentioned that people who wish to remarry had to put their plans on hold to wait for their divorces to be finalized. Also, large weddings weren't allowed for fear of spreading the COVID-19 virus.

***

FAQ - What is a Joint vs. Sole Filing of a Divorce?

There were two options to file for divorce, joint or sole. Sawyer explains in her book, *British Columbia Do Your Own Divorce Kit,* that "In a joint divorce both spouses file jointly... In a sole divorce, one spouse files for the divorce and the other spouse responds." She says joint divorces are the easier option when spouses have lived apart for one year, unless they don't live close by and aren't on speaking terms. Key URL Links are available on the Author's own book website for guidance for Canada, the US, the UK, Australia, and New Zealand at:

breakupmakeuporshakeup.wordpress.com.

Ace and I had a unique set of reasons why I left, just like every couple does. Even within couples there are two stories of why they split up. The main two reasons appear to be cheating and abuse (Krishnan, 2012).

According to Dr. Deborah O'Connor, "Often, it's because they're leaving relationships that have been bad for a long time," (Krishnan, 2012). Neither was the case with us. The decision to separate was one-sided with us, but it can be mutual. Reasons particular to the over 50s that the stories in this book address include:

- **Abuse – At last, a partner is ready to exit an abusive relationship, perhaps after many prior unsuccessful attempts to leave.** For women, once the children have left home, they've received the counselling they needed and have the financial means to leave – they are ready to go. This wasn't our problem, as

Ace is a gentle sweet soul. I'd never hurt him physically either. I couldn't — he's well over six feet tall with the physique of a tennis player — long limbs that could easily push me away.

- **Affair** – One or both of you has found someone that makes you feel alive, youthful and attractive again (a fling), or perhaps someone who seems a better match for the years ahead (a serious affair that threatens your relationship). You can't picture yourself growing older with your current partner and are looking for someone you can grow old with. Maybe, you just want to be alone or have an occasional fling or companion. Again, nope, not that I knew of. Ace has always been faithful and worked in an industry dominated by men. I'm intuitive and never had reason to suspect infidelity. Even if he had been unfaithful, I doubt that it would have been more than a fling. Loyalty and fidelity run deep in his gene pool.

- **Boredom** – Been there done that with that guy/gal, so is this all there is? No, only boring people get bored is my mantra.

- **Disappointment** – Life together just hasn't turned out the way you planned and retirement seems like an endless miserable holiday in perpetual rain. Okay, so we're getting warmer.

- **Fed up** – All those little annoyances over decades add up to the point you can't stand each other anymore. Maybe, you're fed up with her drinking or his cocaine habit, her gambling at the slots or his cheating — you just don't want to spend the rest of your life in conflict. Definitely not, Ace is as offensive as a koala bear.

- **Finances** – That one just never seems to disappear, but unlike your younger years the stakes can be higher. What you do in this last chapter of your life can mean the difference between spending your retirement in front of the TV or living your best days in lovely places. It was irritating in the first few months, that Ace perceived we had to worry about money like we were starving students again, but in actuality we were doing just as well and a bit better than when he was working. When I suggested we put up a greenhouse, he freaked out and suggested we split our finances. I was in shock that he essentially was ending our marriage over a greenhouse. I clarified that I didn't mean an expensive new greenhouse and showed him ideas for turning our raised beds into a greenhouse early in the season. He calmed down, but I was alarmed he was prepared to split up with me over something so petty — some plastic and bamboo stakes. I pointed out that divorcing me would be much more expensive than a greenhouse at any rate.

- **Health issues** – In mid-life it's not uncommon for the Flaccid Fairy to visit your man. Between his erectile dysfunction, your hot flashes courtesy Ms. Menopause, his post-retirement depression and both of your joint replacements there's just no fun in sex anymore. Or, sadly, maybe one of you had a stroke that changed your personality to the point where you can't live together safely. Yes, this was a contributing factor, we had issues in the *boudoir* that we were dealing with that made connecting challenging.

- **Interests** – After the nest is empty, the careers wind down, or you move to a warmer place with a slower pace, couples find they have few or no common interests leading to estrangement Dr. Deborah O'Connor, who studies late-life divorce at UBC, says, "...People look at each other and realize they don't have anything in common anymore, and they're not making each other happy anymore, and they don't want to spent the rest of their lives doing this," (Krishnan, 2012). Sure, I'll own that. Although, our nest has never been full, except for the occasional niblings staying with us while they went to college.

- **Moving** – One of you loves the move to the remote town a far distance from the city when they retired; however, the other feels like they moved to a penal colony. Okay, that may be an overstatement, nevertheless, one of you feels isolated and lonely. Checkmark, another contributing factor that I struggled with and needed to be addressed.

- **Personal growth or lack thereof** – One of you is committed to be your best you, but the other not so much and both of you resent the other for it, or doesn't appreciate or connect with the new you.

Maybe? I think first-borns shouldn't really be allowed to pair up like we did. The only thing that kind of balanced it out is that I'm four years younger than him, or we might have become really competitive. Full disclosure though, I didn't feel quite equal to him until I got a post-graduate degree as well.

- **Power shift** – One partner, who was in a boss position at work, is now retired and decides to be boss of the household when they retire. That doesn't really fly with the stay-at-home partner, who has run the household perfectly well for decades. Myself, I'll concede to giving up 50% control but not 100%. Yup, that definitely was us. More than once when he was working, I would say, "You may be the boss of all those people at work, but you're not the boss of me." What could I say now without hurting his feelings?

- **Priorities** – Differences in priorities can cause rifts, such as one partner wants to focus on time with family but the other wants to focus on time together. If you can't find a balance, this can tear you apart. Tick that box, this was us. His priority was to win programming contests while living in his den. Mine was to have a life together.

- **Retired Husband Syndrome (RHS)** – This is a global phenomenon, for example, in Japan, Grey Divorce has gone "viral" (Dennis, 2016) because of RHS. Suddenly, spouses who don't spend a lot of time together are living around the clock with a stranger who is crowding them into every corner of their home. This makes you completely stressed out about it. The term was first used by Dr. Charles Clifford Johnson, in 1984, to describe female patients, who had a collection of anxiety symptoms upon the retirement of their husbands:

I have frequently heard wives rage with such allegations as, "I am going nuts," "I want to scream," "He is under my feet all the time," "He is driving me crazy," "I'm nervous" or "I can't sleep." These emotional statements are frequently associated with symptoms such as tension headaches, depression, agitation, palpitations, gas, bloating, muscle aches and so forth.

I couldn't find any reference to Retired Wife Syndrome, but I imagine this could happen as well.

Exercise 4. Reasons why we're breaking up

Reflect upon and write why you're breaking up or are considering leaving your spouse. This can be helpful later when you seek legal or counselling help, as they'll want to know the core problems.

In regards to RHS, in North America we can be spoiled by the size of our homes. Unless you live in a micro-suite in Gastown in Vancouver, BC, where they can legally be as small as 200 square feet, although those are meant for one person to occupy, I can imagine it would be even more difficult for a couple to spend all their time together the more restricted the space.

In her book, *Through the Dragon's Gate: Memories of a Hong Kong Childhood,* Jean O'Hara, describes how a family of seven lived in Hong Kong in a 200 square-foot "flat" as a child:

... I shared a bed with my grandmother and younger sister. It was a raised platform. ...we had a straw mat... There was less than one square meter of standing space. A curtain hung from a beam above our heads; when drawn it was the only means of privacy. I grew up unaware I have no privacy, or that seven of us were living in overcrowded conditions. Next door was my parents' bedroom, the only room to have its own door, and a small window, although the partitions did not reach the high ceiling. (O'Hara, 2016, p. 5.)

That sounds unbearably small, especially if everyone was home at the same time.

You don't need to upsize to a sprawling dream house like we did, but a home big enough to accommodate each of the partner's interests makes for a happier couple, than one not big enough for each one's needs and hobbies.

Ace needed enough space for a desk — he got an enormous bonus room over the garage. I needed a woman cave for all my sewing/dyeing/crafting, I got a small bedroom on the main floor. Ace added storage to it, so good enough.

Although, I did suggest that we swap spaces because my little overflowing studio would offer plenty of room for his things — no go.

You don't want a place that's too small either if you're considering cashing out and moving to a less expensive community, for example, our studio apartment in the city of under 500 square feet suits me fine, but when all of us are in it — me, Ace and the Chihuahuas, it's a little tight, unless it's a nice day and we can spill out onto the large patio.

A Sample Separation Agreement

Disclaimer: Best efforts were made to find free, up-to-date and accurate forms and information related to separation, legal separation, divorce from bed and board, limited divorce, and other terms used for when couples live apart from each other for each country. This information is subject to change. Consult legal aid, a lawyer, or do your own Internet search. Be aware that while legislation may say one thing, actual practice can be different.

SAMPLE AGREEMENT INTRODUCTORY CLAUSES:

This full and final agreement was made (date).

BETWEEN: (names and addresses of each party)

Date both parties began living together.

If married, date and location they were married.

Party 1 and Party 2 have been living separate-apart since (date).

Disclosure of whether either party has any children.

INFORMATION ABOUT THIS AGREEMENT:

This agreement addresses: property; debts; details of any past, present or future court proceedings; spousal support (if any) and a dispute resolution-mediation approach to resolve any areas of disagreement, along with termination time of support (Eg: when a party remarries or begins receiving old age pension or dies).

This agreement also contains full disclosure of all assets of both parties; division of family assets such as home, cottage, vehicles, furnishings, pets, bank accounts, pensions, RRSPs, debts, taxes, sharing expenses, etc.

Steps needed to make the agreement work are also outlined for both parties to follow along with dispute resolution details (this can include binding arbitration), especially in the event it's not an uncontested divorce and there are issues.

Canada

There's no such thing as a legal separation in Canada, but being separated from your spouse for a year is grounds for divorce. Separation doesn't mean you have to leave the home you share.

During the pandemic, or any other disaster, leaving the home may be impossible. You can be considered separated when the following criteria apply:

- You move out of the bedroom you shared.

- You start living separate lives.

- You no longer have a sexual relationship.

- You don't go out together for meals or activities.

- You don't share meals together.

- One of you can live on a different floor, or a different room.

In an extremely small space, it would be difficult to prove separation, but not impossible with careful documentation and adherence to the above criteria.

A *Statutory Declaration* form can help document and back up your claim as to the date that you and your partner started your separation.

You can find a Statutory Declaration form for the date your separation started at this link from Service Canada or you can get it from your Service Canada office:

https://catalogue.servicecanada.gc.ca.

US

The 50 states vary greatly in how they deal with the separation of couples.

Not all states recognize legal separation, although they all recognize that couples can draft their own *Separation Agreement* to divide their property and debts.

Some states allow couples to convert their legal separation to a divorce at a later time.

Yet some states require couples who went through a legal separation to start all over again to get divorced:

(www.hg.org/separation-law.html).

The Author's own book website features key URL links to the Separation Guidelines for each of the 50 States.

breakupmakeuporshakeup.wordpress.com.

UK

To apply for a separation download Form D8:

www.gov.uk/government/publications/form-d8-application

Australia

Rather than forms, this website offers helpful information on the effects of separation on partners and their children: http://www.familycourt.gov.au/wps/wcm/connect

New Zealand

Separation application forms can be downloaded, if you both agree to the separation at:

https://www.justice.govt.nz/assets/Documents/Forms.

This same link can also help you access appropriate forms even if only one of you wants to separate.

And again, the Author's own book website features key URL links to the Separation Guidelines for each of these countries and their component provinces or States:

breakupmakeuporshakeup.wordpress.com.

Break Up, Make Up or Shake Up / Cathalynn Labonté-Smith

CHAPTER 2 - Lawyering Up

As I continued my journey, I realized Step 1 for me was to choose a lawyer, because I felt I needed some guidance regarding potential spousal support and my pension.

As I said in *Chapter 1,* perhaps Step 1 should've been to see a counsellor together, even if we wanted to separate.

A good counsellor will be unbiased and remain neutral as to whether you wish to stay together or split up. They're there to help you do whatever you wish to do. A good counsellor also refrains from taking a side with either partner.

The reason to see a lawyer; however, was because I wanted to have all the information before I told Ace what I was planning to do. I only had one shot at settling with my partner, so I had to protect myself and make sure I was adequately provided for. I wanted to cover all my bases. It might not be everyone's Step 1, as lawyers are expensive, but it was mine as I'm a thorough researcher.

It was common sense; however, if a couple divides their assets together in a cooperative way and avoids using lawyers, that they keep all of their assets.

If they end up in conflict in front of a judge in court, the judge will likely split the property 50-50.

The couple pays hefty legal and court costs, and each gets half of whatever is left over after the divorce.

I asked my BFF, who was a family lawyer once upon a time, if she knew of any good family lawyers.

Also, I asked her about divorces, in general, so here are some excerpts from our PM:

> *Me: I was a bit shocked that not all lawyers will give you a free first consultation. Some wanted to charge $300 an hour.*
>
> *Her: Would this be the time to tell you that senior counsel bills around $600 per hour. The questions I would ask a potential lawyer are: How often do you go to Court? Fairway collaborative lawyers would be a good place for you to start.*
>
> *Me: I think there's a niche market for collaborative divorce they offer. They publish their own book called "Clean Break".*
>
> *Her: Also, they have the in-house knowledge base to explain what the laws ARE and what is "usual" in a given case. BC has a collaborative law group in their Bar Association.*
>
> *Those are lawyers committed to NOT going to court at: http://www.collaborativedivorcebc.com/.*
>
> *In Canada, the law about divorce is Federal. Each province has its own property laws. The mechanics of getting divorced (i.e. the paperwork) is individual to each province. But the law that actually does the divorce is federal. Check the court websites in each province--every one of them has their structure and forms*

Three Lawyers

I went to www.lawyerratingz.com and there were hundreds of divorce lawyers to choose from.

To narrow things down, I only looked at lawyers with smiley faces beside their names and who were close by.

In the comments were sad stories, about how unhappy some people were with other lawyers before coming to their present lawyer, and how it cost them hundreds of thousands of dollars.

For the first of the three lawyers I spoke to, I chose one because her clients described her as fair, organized and friendly. Vanessa had that calm energy I was looking for.

And, for the second lawyer, I asked a friend who worked for a law firm if she could recommend someone.

For the third and final lawyer, I chose one close to where I lived. Her corporate website showed that the whole firm was composed of female lawyers.

Government websites have referral lists as well, including legal aid options.

For a full, detailed look at Divorce laws and guides for Canada, the US, the UK, Australia and New Zealand, please go to the Author's book website:

breakupmakeuporshakeup.wordpress.com

Three Surprises

I contacted each of the three firms I picked and was met with three surprises:

1. **Before scheduling an appointment, they conduct a conflict of interest check to see if my spouse was already being represented by them.** That'd be quite the surprise, since Ace had no idea I was leaving him.

2. **Not all first consultations are free.** In fact, only Vanessa offered a free first consultation to me. The second lawyer charged $250/hour for the first consultation. I couldn't get the lawyer I originally requested. The third lawyer charged $300/hour for the first consultation, but the fee would be applied to legal costs if you went with her firm.

3. **An intake form must be filled out before the appointment.** Each of the forms they sent me asked for different information than the other firms. Each form took at least an hour to fill out this Law Firm Intake Questionnaire.

After I filled out the forms and sent them back, it took about a week for the firms to get back to me.

It all seemed like a long drawn out process just to get in the door, especially with those firms charging hundreds of dollars for the privilege of me interviewing them.

***

Law Firm Intake Questionnaire

As I experienced, when you contact a lawyer to pursue a divorce, you'll need to fill out an intake questionnaire providng a wealth of personal information and details relating to your case.

To start, you'll be providing your full legal name, maiden name or surname prior to marriage, photo ID, your marital status prior to your current marriage, birth date, contact information for yourself and your spouse or common-law partner and for any lawyers either of you may have been in touch with.

As well you'll need to provide your social insurance number, date-place of marriage, marriage certificate (if applicable), date of separation, whether there has been cohabitation since separation, details of any prior separations, reasons for separation, details concerning any children, financial support provided to them and any proposed support for the children.

You'll also need to provide details of any employment for yourself and your partner, including employer, gross and net income, health benefits etc. If you're retired, then details of any pensions would be provided.

As well, you'll need to list all assets, including family residence, owners on title and approximate value of your home; any other real estate owned, such as a cottage; any mortgages and amounts concerning your real estate holdings; value of your vehicles and any other owned items of value.

If you have a business, the value of this would also be provided. Assets also include bank accounts and balances, any investments, retirement plans, pension plans, insurance plans and any other assets of value.

You'll also need to provide information on any and all debts you each have, including credit cards, loans, lines of credit and overdrafts, and any other debts.

Estate planning details are also needed, including information on any wills.

SAFETY: There is also a degree of screening for family violence, so you'll need to disclose if you're afraid of your partner and reasons for your answers.

You'll also need to divulge if the police have been involved with your family in any way and details of this.

As well, you'll need to say if you're comfortable meeting with your partner in the same room and if not, state the reasons why.

You'll also need to outline any concerns you may have regarding the safety of your children, and provide any concerns you may have regarding your partner's mental and emotional health, violence and any alcohol or drug abuse concerns.

FAQ - What is a Divorce?

Divorce in North America, and many other continents, is the legal dissolution of a marriage by a court. Prior to July of 2019 when it was made illegal to do so in India, Muslim men could use the highly controversial method of triple *taliq* to divorce. Any Muslim man needed only to declare to his wife verbally, or in writing, email, or text, "I divorce you, I divorce you, I divorce you," to instantly, legally and irrevocably divorce his spouse.

FAQ - What is a Collaborative Divorce?

A collaborative divorce according to the BC Government website is a ". . .law process is to settle your case fairly, without going to court. The lawyers are hired to reach a settlement, not to go to court." Collaborative divorce is an option for those couples who want a DIY style separation/divorce and don't need a lot of lawyering. Key URL links are available on the author's own book website for guidance for Canada, the US, the UK, Australia, and New Zealand at:

breakupmakeuporshakeup.wordpress.com

***

FAQ - Do I Need a Lawyer?

As far as DIY separations and divorces go, Sawyer in *Do Your Own Divorce Kit for British Columbia* advises that you don't make a lack of money the reason for not getting a divorce. She says that most divorces are uncontested, so you don't really need a lawyer if you're willing to invest your own time in filling out the provided forms. However, if you're in the 15% of cases that have a contested divorce you will need to consult with a lawyer. Sawyer says good candidates for a DIY divorce are where:

- You've been separated for the legally required amount of time.

- There are no children to arrange custody or support for.

● Neither spouse needs financial support from the other.

● All property is divided and both spouses are happy with the property settlement.

● The only remaining task is to ask the court to make an order to file for the divorce.

***

Exercise 5. Lawyers to contact:

Write down the names and contact information including phone numbers and email addresses of lawyers you wish to contact. Friends might have referrals or check out online reviews of the best divorce lawyers in your area. Even if you decide to do your own divorce using a kit, it's still valuable to get a free or low-cost consultation.

Exercise 6. Questions for My Lawyer:

Questions can include: Do I really need to get a divorce or is a *Separation Agreement* all I need?

How much will the divorce cost?

Can I do some of the process myself to cut down on costs? If so, what parts?

What are my rights?

Can I get spousal support? If so, when can I get spousal support?

Can I get child support? If so, when can I get spousal support?

When does legal separation start?

Am I allowed to stay in my home?

How can I get my spouse to leave our home?

What is an Arbitrator?

What is a Collaborative Divorce?

Can I get divorced with a kit?

Can you walk me through the divorce process?

How long will the divorce take?

I don't want my spouse to know I'm planning to leave them, how do I pay you when we have joint accounts and the same credit card?

What is the next step?

Exercise 7. Leaving Day

Keep this plan secure where your partner won't find it, if you're afraid of your abusive partner or you don't want them to know of your plans. (Write on a piece of paper or computer.)

My Plan to Leave is (detail your plan in full):

I will inform the following people that I am leaving and/ OR when asking my partner to leave for safety, OR I will ask the following people to be with me at the time; I will take the following with me; Childcare plan: Pet and/or livestock care plan; Contact list.

Exercise 8.   Parting Checklist

In many ways, you're starting a whole new life and there are a myriad of potential things to see to, including: Changing the name of your Will beneficiary and Life Insurance beneficiary and Power of Attorney.

You may need-want to change your name; close bank accounts and open new ones, change address and contact information; redirect mail; update passport, driver's license, health insurance card and more – so write down a list and add to it to keep on top of these changes.

Exercise 9.   My First Year of Transition:
Write down your goals, activities and plans for your first year of transition through separation/divorce.

FAQ - How Much Will My Divorce Cost?

You can get DIY divorce kits and just pay for the court filing fees for your documents and save thousands.

 Although, you may find out later you've neglected to account for something, such as your partner's pension, spousal support payments, or they may have managed to hide an asset in another province/state or country, and you may end up losing out on your fair share of something.

Usually, an initial retainer needs to be paid if you use a lawyer. It is held in trust and then billed monthly.

If you do as much of the prep work yourselves as you can, like filling out the intake form completely, or drafting the *Separation Agreement,* perhaps a divorce could set you back between $3,000-$10,000 all in. A huge range, but when/if you speak to a lawyer, they can give you a ballpark figure at the end of your first consultation.

Some firms offer a flat rate for an uncontested separation agreement and divorce, whether or not children are involved.

But as soon as there is any back and forth, it switches to an hourly rate that varies from firm to firm.

***

FAQ - Do Common-law Couples Need to Get a Divorce?

Couples who opt out of marriage don't need a divorce, in most cases. However, they may still need a formal agreement to divide assets when there is property involved, or they share custody of children—or pets—so it's best to consult a lawyer about your situation.

***

Collaborative Divorce Resources

If you are concerned about your safety if your partner were to discover what's in your browser history, see the FAQ - How Do I Keep My Partner from Knowing What I've Looked at on My Browser? in the *Introduction*.

Disclaimer: Best efforts were made to find free, up-to-date and accurate forms and information related to collaborative divorce for each country. This information is subject to change. Consult legal aid, a lawyer, or do your own Internet search. Be aware that while legislation may say one thing the actual practice can be much different.

Canada:

As divorce is a provincial or territorial matter, please consult your province or territory's government website and then refine your search to obtain collaborative divorce guidelines and information.

You can also obtain further such information via family law lawyers in your province or territory. In addition, the Author's own website provides an impressive list of URL links to Collaborative Divorce advice:

breakupmakeuporshakeup.wordpress.com

US:

As divorce is a State matter, please consult your State government website and then refine your search to obtain collaborative divorce guidelines and information. You can also obtain further such information via family law lawyers in your State. In addition, the Author's own website provides an impressive list of URL links to Collaborative Divorce advice.

UK:

Divorce in the United Kingdom is largely governed by the UK's component countries.

Please consult the websites for England & Wales; Scotland; and, Northern Ireland, and then refine your search to obtain collaborative divorce guidelines and information. You can also obtain further such information via family law lawyers in your component country.

In addition, the Author's own website has a list of URL links to Collaborative Divorce advice for England & Wales; Scotland, and, Northern Ireland.

Australia

Visit the government website and search for information on collaborative divorce law.

New Zealand

Visit the government website and search for information on collaborative divorce law for all of these countries:

breakupmakeuporshakeup.wordpress.com

Next, we'll take a break from my own journey to look at a case history – the story of James and his divorce experiences.

CHAPTER 3: James' Story:
Everything I Do

One divorce veteran I turned to in a time when I was overwhelmed was my trusted friend James. He said:

> *You need a lawyer who doesn't need the money, who likes you, wants to represent you, and is efficient; that's hard to find, so you have to see a lot of them.*

> *An expensive lawyer may be more efficient and do things in less time than a less expensive lawyer that takes more time, so the more experienced, higher-priced lawyer may be less expensive in the long-run. It's not just my experience but the experience of many people I know who have been through the same situation.*

> *If you're in a hurry, you'll pay big time. You want a calm divorce. Just be calm and forget about it. Split your assets and don't fight.*

James put a lot of time into interviewing several lawyers, much more than I did. He found just the right one to take on his case because it involved the custody of his child.

James was single for about 12 years after his divorce from his first wife — before he was introduced to Chelsea by friends. His friends touted her as a perfect match for him. She was a gorgeous young model and enjoyed the things James did, such as diving, sailing and parties.

They lived together happily for two years, although there were red flags when she began to isolate him from his friends and stir up trouble with his family members.

James already had an adult child from his first marriage and at 40 years-old, he didn't want to start another family. He was ready to enjoy mid-life freedom with his beautiful new partner. He was also going through a career transition, so he didn't feel it was a good time to have a family.

This relationship was definitely not on a "family plan." James also wanted a partner who was financially independent. She bragged about her wealth from her work as a model. To him, it seemed like their long-term goals were aligned.

Chelsea started to talk about getting married. He wasn't in a hurry to go through another marriage, but neither did he think it was a bad idea as he didn't want to be lonely again. She got "pushy" about being married, so he agreed.

On their honeymoon, a harsh wake-up call began for him, "Suddenly, I was living with someone who was no longer interested in me, she was critical of my friends, and I found out she was broke." The interests he thought they shared stopped, so did their sex life. He hoped things would work out when they went back home to the West Coast to their new home.

The financial strain began right away. She couldn't cover her share of the mortgage.

"I gave her money to start businesses, in hopes things would get better. In the ultimate move of stupidity, I gave her access to my bank accounts," he recounts. He hoped that her ventures would succeed.

Chelsea's friend had a baby. She told James that she wanted one. He was concerned because she wasn't the motherly type. Chelsea drank a bottle-to-a-bottle-and-a-half of wine daily.

Even though the timing was bad, as her spending and their new businesses were straining their finances, he caved in to her request.

She got pregnant right away and was convinced it was going to be a girl. The test results came to their home from the lab and they opened them together. The baby was a boy. She had a melt-down.

"She had inconsolable angst about it being a boy. From that moment on we struggled," he said. In the months that followed, he went through life as normal: going to work, paying bills. She gave birth to a healthy boy and he found himself loving being a father to a baby again.

Until one day he bought groceries and his bank card was declined. He went home and checked his bank accounts — all their savings were gone.

"She did her typical 'she needed money for her business' story, but this time it had gone too far because I no longer had money for the mortgage — the cupboards were bare." He had a new baby, limited funds, and Chelsea teetered on bankruptcy but wasn't stopping her spending. He was about to lose his house, his business was struggling, and his marriage was failing.

He went to his accountant and said, "She won't stop spending. What do I do?"

The accountant's response was, "What can you do?" Chelsea had a spending addiction.

Ultimately, James discovered the extent of the bills, including a line of credit and previously unknown credit cards in both their names. The company he was working for closed its doors, and he had to sell the house to pay her bills.

Within a year, they moved back east to start over but that didn't help their financial problems, so he moved back to the West Coast to be closer to his job in the US, but he lost that job. She was still over-spending, so he paid off her credit cards.

"This is the last time I'm paying off your credit cards," he told her.

"We're getting divorced," she said the next day.

He was relieved. There was no intimacy left in the relationship. Even after they were separated, her excessive spending haunted him.

Their things were in storage and he went to the locker. By coincidence a moving truck arrived when he was there. It was already full of thousands of dollars of new furniture but had arrived to pick up things from the locker to add to the van.

He called Chelsea and asked her where she got the money for the new furniture when she'd told him she was broke. She gave him the usual denial.

In their nine years of marriage, she went through his life savings, plus costly lawyer's fees over the three years it took to settle the custody arrangements.

In his 50s when the divorce came through, he was starting all over again. James' ex seems to have been looking for someone to take care of her financially to enable her shopping addiction.

Chelsea tried to get full custody of their son, but never produced any proof of him being an unfit father. In fact, he was the one changing diapers, cooking meals, taking his son to preschool, and working full-time to pay the bills.

On one occasion, James was going to take his son for a vacation to a tropical island, but she refused to give written consent for him to take the boy, so James went to court.

When the judge asked her why she wouldn't give consent she said, "Because he won't bring him back."

"What do you do for a living?" the judge asked James.

"I'm a biochemist," he replied.

"Can you do that on a tropical island with no one around?" asked the judge.

"No," responded James.

"Yes, he can," insisted Chelsea.

"That sounds like a great holiday. I'd like to go on a holiday like that. I'm going to allow this," said the judge.

Chelsea continued to say and do whatever she could to make the divorce hell, even though she'd been the who demanded it.

The lowest point for James was arriving at his son's school one morning to find him in tears. When James asked him what was wrong, his son said, "Mommy said I'll never see you again."

At one point, they went to court and Chelsea brought along a film crew to the courthouse with the intent of making a movie about their breakup. James' lawyer asked the film crew what they were doing there. They left.

By the time they were divorced, Chelsea was living with another man and pregnant.

After the 24-hour mandatory waiting period after the divorce was finalized she remarried.

"I feel like the guy did me a huge favour. I feel like I should buy him presents every day," says James. He feels that now he's in his 50s, it takes longer to get over relationships versus in his 20s when they were about having fun.

One evening when we were working on our writing projects at his place, it was getting late and I felt chilled. I asked for a blanket, but instead he brought me a goose down duvet and tucked it around me, then he brought me an Earl Grey tea with honey.

"James, you're a nurturer. You've been with women who take advantage of that side of you," I said.

He agreed that his second wife and his last serious girlfriend were both controlling women. He feels:

> *They used me as a healing conduit, rather than as a true lover. I feel wiser now that I can see things*

coming. I feel with great sadness that I didn't find the love of my life in my 20s to live out our lives together. I'm more cynical about relationships, more cautious. But I know I still have all of that in me.

****

Ace and I had the kind of relationship James dreamed about, where you meet when you're young, fall in love and are there for each other for a long time. I hadn't thought of it like that before.

****

James and I met again at a cheerful coffee shop. The barista greeted him warmly, as everyone does. He's one of those magnetic yet humble people whom everyone is attracted to. He works in a field where you need to be able to create a rapport with people quickly.

He talked briefly about his childhood. His parents split when he was young.

"Being a priority was not part of the equation with my parents," he said. He's made his son his top priority in his life. In many ways, this time in his life in his late 50s is "the best time ever," as:

Intimacy is better, communication is better. The character of your partner is more developed.

There are so many pleasures in knowing someone you're with is real versus a 30-year-old and I have all this freedom. Being alone feels good to me. I don't want to be alone, but I don't want someone depending on me for their emotional well-being.

The main stumbling block is the issue of trust: he finds it can be "very hurtful" when women act completely out of character. He finds himself being analytical when it comes to dating. He asks himself:

- *Am I attracted to this woman?*

- *Do I trust her?*

- *Am I going to be in love with her?*

In addition to over-analyzing a relationship before it starts, he also finds himself flooded with too much memory of past pain to pursue someone. Like someone looking at a potential partner through a pane of glass and knowing how much it'll hurt if you go through the shards to meet them, so you pass by not taking that risk.

He's waiting for something "magical and miraculous yet simple" to happen. Someone he has a sense of "destiny" with.

To people who are having problems with their relationships he says, "Take your time, let it be, find a therapist."

James was headed for a secure and early retirement until the financial disaster of this second marriage, the bankruptcy and divorce.

His son is now in high-school and James is 60 years-old.

James was back on track for retirement until COVID-19 when he lost his job. He has an abundance of skills, talents and contacts. He should have a new position by the time you read this.

Is the moral of this story to be financially secure don't get divorced? Not at all. Unhappiness just isn't worth that price.

But if, like James, you're married to an over spender, you may have no other option.

Is the take-away, never to get married?

You could just live with someone, right?

But in some countries, if you live common-law for even a year, you have all the legal rights of a married couple, including a partner being entitled to 50% of the estate when a couple breaks up, unless you have an airtight *Cohabitation Agreement* to protect yourself.

***

FAQ - What are the Differences between Cohabitation, Prenup, Postnup & Separation Agreements?

A *Cohabitation Agreement* is written and signed before or during living together or marriage. If you have a home, and other assets to protect for future security, this can be good relationship insurance.

This type of agreement outlines in the case of a breakup how you will divide your property and debts, as well as what you will do if you can't agree, such as use a meditator.

However, the agreement can't include custody decisions. All four agreements are outlined in the following chart on the next page:

Agreement	When	What it may include
Cohabitation	Before or during common-law or legal marriage. Used for non-traditional relationships, (Eg: same-sex or polyamorous). Can't be created after a married couple separates, then a Separation Agreement is created according to your local separation laws.	Division of property and debt. Spousal support. How disputes will be handled. Can't include custody of children Custody of pets. Wills and estates.
Prenuptial	Before legal marriage	Division of property and debt. Spousal support. How disputes will be handled. Custody of children from prior relationships. Wills and estates.
Postnuptial or Marriage Agreement	During a marriage	Division of property and debt. Spousal support. How disputes will be handled. Custody of children from prior relationships. Custody of pets. Wills and estates.
Separation	When couples in legal marriages separate and don't have any prior agreement in place.	Division of property and debt. Spousal support. How disputes will be handled. Custody of children and pets. Wills and estates.

The different types of agreements can be confusing, but hopefully the previous table describing at what stage they are used and what terms are included if the relationship fails, clarified them for you.

Danielle Dubé in her article, *Should you get a prenup or cohabitation agreement before settling down?,* reports that prenups are rare and *Cohabitation Agreements* are even rarer.

She says the reasons to have such agreements are to protect the wealth and property you bring into a relationship, shield yourself from your partner's debt, and to make custody of children you bring with you from a previous partnership clear.

However, if you are a young couple in your first committed relationship, it's hard to predict what the circumstances of your union will be years later.

These agreements can be expensive to have a lawyer draft, so a young couple has to decide if it's worth the outlay for a document that may not serve their needs decades later if ever.

***

You can maintain separate households, but it can be tricky if not impossible to keep a relationship going when you maintain two households.

James tried that option with his next serious relationship.

But with his partner having her brood to raise and him having his son to raise, it was logistically, physically and emotionally impossible to build a long-lasting relationship spread across two cities.

***

FAQ – Separation During Self-Quarantine?

Yes, you could be separated from your partner, either married or common law, even when neither of you can leave the premises, such as during a quarantine due to a pandemic or other causes, provided you can meet the terms that determine separation, such as not sharing a bed, having a sexual relationship with each other, going out as a couple socially, having meals together, or engaging in other couple activities.

During the pandemic some couples remained living together even after their separation or Covidivorce was complete.

In Brooklynn Neustaeter's article *Living with an Ex: When Pandemic Breakups Don't Mean Separating,* a Canadian couple, who completed their *Separation Agreement* still lived together because the real estate market was frozen.

The man couldn't find a place to buy.

Other reasons exes couldn't physically leave were due to quarantining from family, maintaining social bubbles, and the logistics of even looking at properties.

The pandemic also brought some exes back together. People reached out to their former partners over social media and by texting out of loneliness, curiosity, or regret that they broke up with them years ago.

***

Living without partnering up is something I could see myself doing for a while, but not forever. I'm just not wired that way.

Even a friend who swore she'd never get married again after her divorce eventually found herself going down the aisle a second time.

Sue Johnson in her book *Hold Me Tight*, says that we need to have an emotional reliance on our intimate partner:

> *This drive to emotionally attach. . .is wired into our genes and our bodies.*
>
> *It is as basic to life, health, and happiness as the drives for food, shelter, or sex.*
>
> *We need emotional attachments with a few irreplaceable others to be physically and mentally healthy — to survive...*

CHAPTER 4: Tara's Story – Better Off Alone

I met up with another divorce warrior, my friend Tara. She's a hard-working woman who's been struggling to complete her divorce for many years.

We met for lunch and I told her my news. She was surprised and sad for us, just like I was when many years ago she told me that she and her husband were splitting up.

Tara and Leo were the darlings of our neighbourhood.

They hosted many parties in their lovely home. Leo worked at the airport nearby and was able to get flights at no cost through the airline he worked for. He attended international mountain biking events.

Tara worked as a legal secretary downtown and was always beautifully dressed and well groomed.

But they could barely afford the mortgage on that idyllic home. The travel costs for Leo's cycling aside from the flights were out of pocket and he quickly racked up a lot of consumer debt.

Their lifestyles were unbalanced with Leo traveling the world pursuing his passion, whereas Tara worked long days bringing a bagged lunch that she ate at her desk to keep the creditors at bay and raising their son on her own.

Their son was a budding scholar and athlete. Tara did her own manicures and shopped at consignment stores to keep herself looking as professional as the other ladies in the firm. She was happy to support Leo's fitness, but was concerned about the debt.

She warned Leo about the mounting credit card debt. He ignored her and booked yet another trip. She would've been wise to unjoin herself from their joint credit card and line of credit (LOC) debt at this time, but she didn't.

Tara could no longer keep them afloat and when Leo got back from his trip, she broke the news that they were going to have to put their house up for sale.

They sold their bungalow and found an old, neglected rental house in the neighbourhood. They didn't have to pay property taxes anymore, so they were able to pay off their large line of credit and were mortgage-free.

They saved for their son's post-secondary education. He had scholarships for his undergraduate degree, but they'd have to cover his living expenses so their son wouldn't have the burden of student loans.

The couple put all they could save into the government Registered Education Savings Plan (RESP) that matched parental savings. Leo still spent his time off with his mountain biking buddies, leaving most of the household responsibilities to Tara.

One day an invitation came to her email inbox for her high-school reunion. She usually deleted such invitations, but she could stay with family when she got there and drop in on her son at his university.

Tara looked amazing at the reunion with her long dark hair freshly cut and highlighted, and her black lace dress showing off her legs. She had a glass of sparkling wine in her hand. Her old high-school sweetheart, Alex, found her in the crowd by her familiar pretty laugh.

Alex was a widower. Tara extended her stay, so that she could spend more time with Alex. She soon moved in with him into his large modern home.

At first, she told Leo that she had stayed because her aunt was unwell. Eventually, she broke the news to him that she wasn't coming back because she was unhappy.

She found a new job in her old home-town.

Tara and Alex enjoyed golfing together. Things were great, although his grown children didn't approve of the relationship. She suspected they were concerned for their inheritances. The tension got to be too much for Tara and affected her relationship with Alex as he sided with his children. She returned home.

She asked Leo if she could retrieve her things from the house. Leo was angry about the affair, but also happy to see his wife again. He asked if she wanted to move back in with him, share the rent and try to reconcile. She tells us what happened from there:

> *I felt awkward. I was so full of guilt. After nine months, we grew apart again. I got back in contact with the person whom I originally had my affair with. However, it was only by telephone and emails. We never saw each other again in person. After one full year, Leo and I both knew this was over and we officially separated.*

> *Divorce proceedings started, but he refused to cooperate with my equal part of monies of pension of the 32 years of marriage. He put all responsibility and cost on my end of our divorce. He makes more money than me, and it's been a long, slow process for me to finally get what's equally and rightfully mine—half the pension. The lawyer representing me once told me that] he or she with the most money wins, so I continue to squirrel away my money and hopefully get the procedure done before I'm 65 so I can peacefully retire gracefully.*

Over the next few years, Tara took in a friend, Jordan, who'd suffered a devastating loss. His wife had died due to cancer. What started out as a roommate arrangement eventually became a common-law partnership.

Then things changed. Jordan stopped contributing to the rent and grocery money. He spent his money on booze and meals out for himself.

Jordan didn't help around the apartment, and on his days off, of which there were many because he was on sick leave, he left the apartment looking like a disaster zone.

It seems Jordan didn't have any limits on his behaviour. He drank in excess and would become violent.

He once choked her to the point she thought she was going to die. She was able to get out from under his bulk and run out of their apartment for help.

The police arrested Jordan for assault and a restraining order was issued.

After that incident, Jordan went into rehabilitation offered through his work. He managed to convince Tara that he'd pay his fair share of the rent and expenses, and promised he'd never hurt her again.

She gave him a trial period and he turned out to be a model roommate for the first few months. But soon the pattern of drinking, skipping work, and abusing her started again.

On her birthday, she got dressed up and took herself out for a good dinner with a glass of wine.

When she got home, she found a birthday card from the dollar store on the table with the words, "Love, Jordan," carelessly scrawled inside and a candy bar next to it. That was the last straw for her.

She left him a note telling him he needed to be out by the first of the month or she would call the authorities. She had wisely not put his name on the lease. He was out after four days.

Tara did a really brave thing by standing up for herself and getting rid of her abuser. She took him back when he stopped drinking, but when he started drinking again she made him leave.

Throughout her ordeal with Jordan, she continued to persist with her divorce from Leo.

After 15 years of expensive lawyer's bills the divorce is final. It was worth the investment in time and money, because she has security from half of his pension when for her retirement.

Tara is now a doting grandmother. She's happy on her own. The self-quarantine was challenging as she spent months alone in her apartment, but it was better than being in a financially, verbally, and physically abusive relationship.

***

FAQ - How Long does Divorce Take?

This is one of those questions like how long is a piece of string? The answer is it depends on the factors such as:

- Complexity of the couple's holdings both domestic and foreign.

- Cooperativeness of partners. If the couple has little in the way of accumulated assets and are both highly motivated to end the union after the separation, during which a *Separation Agreement* was carried out splitting assets and debts, an uncontested divorce could be finalized within three or four months. This is the best-case scenario. Although, throw in a second or third wave of the pandemic or some other disaster that shuts down the court system and it could be more months or years of waiting.

- Whether or not the divorce is uncontested or contested. An uncontested divorce means both partners agree to the divorce, whereas a contested divorce means one of the partners is unwilling to agree to the divorce. In some countries, you can still get divorced in a contested divorce after a period of time. Things can get messy, more expensive and more drawn out. For example, if there's a property that has liens against it and there's a lawsuit pending against the jointly owned property, partners have to wait for that lawsuit to be settled before their assets can be divided. It could take a couple of years, five years, ten years or until one of the partners dies, but those are worst-case scenarios. Also, some partners evade court dates drawing out the process and ratcheting up costs.

- Every country and the state or province within it has a different waiting period and protocol once the divorce is filed, but once you reach that waiting period, be it three months or a year, your divorce will be finalized.

- In 2020, the pandemic backed up the courts, because they were closed for many months because they weren't prepared to operate with virtual online hearings.

Coming up in the next chapter: A look at my own divorce process and costs-details involved.

CHAPTER 5 – My Divorce

After hearing the grisly details of some of my friends' divorces, I wondered if things would turn ugly for Ace and I?

The day of my lawyer's appointment arrived.

I wish I'd arranged to bring a close friend along.

Once I was in the sleek law office, the receptionist gave me yet another form and asked for my ID to photocopy.

At last, I met with Vanessa, the first lawyer I picked from the Internet, got settled in with coffee and started to feel at ease.

I brought a list of my most burning questions ahead of time. Before seeing a lawyer, please also review earlier information on Questions to ask your Lawyer – and jot down those uppermost questions in your mind.

***

Burning Divorce Questions

Vanessa wanted to hear why I was there and why I was leaving my spouse. We went over the intake form together, then it was my turn to ask questions.

- **What do I need to pay up front and how will I be billed?** I wanted a rough estimate and to find out if they had a flat fee option. It was hard for her to give me an estimate, but it could be up to $10,000 for a straightforward case. Less, if we were amicable and did much of the work ourselves.

- **How often do you go to court?** I know this isn't necessarily a reflection of the skill of the lawyer, but it could give me an idea of her personal practice.

- **If our case got to court, what kind of outcomes have you seen in cases similar to ours?** She might not have a similar enough case, but it wouldn't hurt to ask.

- **Do you specialize in divorce?** Vanessa was listed as a Family Law lawyer but I double-checked.

- **What is your tendency in resolution?** I wanted someone who wasn't going to get Ace's back up. I was looking at the long-term goal of staying friends. I didn't want a lawyer who would ramp him up and make this into a conflict situation. So I needed her to tell me her approach. She said there were other ways to reach an agreement if needed, such as mediation and arbitration, as well escalations to court.

- **Will I be dealing with you or a colleague?** It's been my past experience of dealing with lawyers for real estate, wills and other matters, to be passed off to junior associates, paralegals, and legal secretaries. These team members can be helpful and charge out at lower rates. However, I wanted to know that when it mattered a senior lawyer would be the one doing the job for me, not a junior lawyer. I had to ask that.

- **How available are you?** This is an area that lawyers receive the most complaints about, because they're exceedingly busy professionals and can't always get back to their clients as quickly as they'd like. I like to hear back within a day, so I'd want to know if she provides an emergency number.

- **What advice do you have for me to save on legal fees?** Vanessa gave me some suggestions, including discussing settlement options between ourselves.

- **Can I stop at Separation?** I had in my mind that we'd be like other people we knew who were separated and just never bothered completing the big "D" by officially getting divorced.

Vanessa recommended we make a clean break of it.

She reassured me that the divorce part was the easiest part of the separation.

Vanessa suggested other reasons to divorce at the end of the one-year period. For example, because of our ages, not getting a divorce brings up estate issues if one of us dies.

Divorce is the simplest cleanest option after a full year of separation. It wraps up the marriage and also allows for the equalization of Canadian Pension Plan (CPP).

The only reasons to not separate would be for religious beliefs, or for health insurance benefits.

- **Before I leave.** What were my next steps? In my particular case, she suggested I do the following:

  o Tell Ace I was separating from him and discuss how we wanted to divide our assets

  o Keep the *status quo* as much as possible until we signed a formal agreement.

At the end of the meeting, I had a much better sense of what I needed to do next. Most importantly, I needed to tell Ace of my intent to separate and eventually divorce. I'd do that the next time I saw him in person. I also wanted to download the online *Separation Agreement* form and lay out some terms for discussion between us.

Follow-up Steps

Vanessa was just like I thought she would be — keen and kind. She answered all my questions that I had prepared and then some. She spent 90 minutes with me and didn't charge me for the extra time, like some lawyers do. I left Vanessa's office feeling calmer and with a plan.

I cancelled my appointments with the two lawyers who wanted big money for a first consultation.

It only took me a few hours to fill out the *Separation Agreement* to present to Ace, because I'd gathered our information for all those intake forms.

Ace video chatted with me that evening and was pressing me about when I was coming home. I broke the news to him that I'd seen a lawyer and wanted to separate. He was surprised and not surprised. He made it clear that's not what he wanted.

I emailed the draft *Separation Agreement* to Ace and said that we could discuss it next time I came over. He wanted to know my timeline. I said there was no timeline, that I wasn't in any hurry, and we could take this at a pace that was comfortable for him.

His immediate concern was what to do with things that neither of us would have room for in smaller homes. I promised I'd find a home for the piano and other items, and not shirk my responsibilities to sell or rehome things.

He asked if I would wait a year to complete the *Separation Agreement.* I was fine with that. As far as what to do with the house, he wanted to eventually sell the place.

Now that I'd moved out, talked to a lawyer, and told Ace my intentions to separate from him I felt like the hardest part was over. After the year's grace period that he'd asked for, we could go back and forth on the *Separation Agreement* by email, then when we were in agreement take it to our respective lawyers, or if necessary, a mediator, before signing off on it.

A mediator is a person trained to help a couple reach an agreement. A mediator listens to both parties and helps them reach a solution. If the couple cannot reach a mutually agreed upon solution, then they can go back to their lawyers, or arbitrator. Perhaps, their lawyers will hire an arbitrator, or they can go to court. Many lawyers are also mediators.

Another option is to use an arbitrator, an independent person appointed or hired to settle a dispute between a married or common-law couple. The arbitrator can work with the couple and their lawyers at any point in the uncoupling process. An arbitrator is different from a mediator, because the arbitrator will settle a dispute between couple via arbitration decisions that are legally binding, whereas the mediator listens to both parties and helps them negotiate a mutually agreed upon solution (See Chapter 20 for detailed information on Mediators and Arbitrators).

I didn't think we'd need a mediator, an arbitrator, or the extreme measure of the courtroom and judge, but you never know if things might turn sour during a breakup.

As a Canadian, I could stay in the marital house and still be separated, as long as we no longer shared the same bedroom and didn't sleep together, didn't have meals together, or didn't attend social events together. Hey, that sounded like regular married life (just kidding). According to Sawyer's *Do Your Own Divorce Kit*,

> *You can live in the same house as your spouse if you conducted your life completely separately, although it is much easier to prove this ground if you can say that one person lived in separately locked and inaccessible living quarters.*

Even though the country home was large enough to do that, I wanted to be in the city amongst my long-time friends and other writers. While my husband was happily nesting in the country after all those years of business travel.

Yes, I'd miss my spacious home and yard in the country. We'd have to work out some visitation arrangement with the dogs. If Ace was really going to move to Alberta, we could each take one. One of the dogs was a present from my parents to me. The other one I gave to him for his birthday.

***

FAQ - How Can I See a Lawyer Without My Partner Knowing?

Not all lawyers will give you a free first consultation for a separation or divorce. They may charge you by the hour or a flat rate for the consultation but give it back to you as credit if you hire them for your case.

If you need money for a lawyer, and/or if you don't want your spouse to know you're seeing a lawyer:

1. Go to lawyers that don't charge for the first consultation.

2. Go to legal aid to see if you qualify for assistance. They have strict guidelines but every case is reviewed.

3. Ask for cash back at places like grocery stores when you make other purchases and pay the lawyer in cash.

4. Pawn something of value, (a collateral loan) or sell something, like jewellery, maybe your wedding ring, electronics, musical instruments, antiques, or collections.

5. Ask someone for a short-term loan, like family or close friends.

***

FAQ - What Are the Steps to Divorce?

The steps to a divorce aren't necessarily linear. People go back and forth to their partners sometimes.

What starts out as a tiff and spending one night in the guestroom can evolve into a year-long separation and then a divorce.

Or, you pick up and leave with the kids in the night, spend a couple of weeks in a hotel, and then he or she persuades you to come back.

Things are fine until you have another blow out, rinse, repeat often until the kids have left home and you finally break free. However, the process usually is:

1. Separation for a period of time, for example, a year for a no-fault divorce in Canada. This can be done within the same home depending on the laws of your country. If there's an extreme emergency circumstance, such as abuse or an affair that there is evidence for, this waiting period might be able to be waived and you may be able to file for divorce sooner.

2. Complete a written *Separation Agreement* signed by the partners. This agreement outlines how you will divide your assets, property, investments, earnings both present and future, such as pensions

and businesses, and debts, like a LOC, credit cards, and personal loans from the in-laws. Also, a schedule of child, spousal and pet/livestock custody arrangement and support agreements are included in the agreement. If you are in a common-law relationship this is the end of the process. Many married couples choose not to file for divorce after they split their assets, for reasons of religious beliefs, the cost of divorce, or so benefits can be maintained.

3. Filing for a divorce with the court after the separation period ends.

4. The divorce is filed with the court and once accepted a decree is sent to you when it's finalized.

FAQ - What is a *Separation Agreement*?

A *Separation Agreement* is a document sometimes drafted by the separating couple themselves, or with the help of a mediator, arbitrator, or their lawyers, that outlines the division of their property, income and debts. It may also include child, spousal and pet and livestock custodial and support agreements.

If you are in a common-law relationship, in many countries, signing this agreement and following through with what's contained in it is the end of the uncoupling process. A divorce isn't necessary, though a couple may be motivated to do so to obtain greater closure or if they wish to remarry and it also clarifies inheritances. See Chapter 18 for further details on Separation.

CHAPTER 6: Paolo's Story:
You Need to Calm Down

Same-sex couples aren't immune from the problems that mixed-sex couples experience.

My friend, Paolo, needed a sharp lawyer to get his fair share of the house he and his partner once shared.

Delaying the sale of the shared home can make sense if exes are amicable and it lets the value of the property rise, such as in the case of the pandemic stalling the market. Continuing to share the house worked for several years for Paola and his ex until it didn't.

Paolo liked distinguished looking older gentlemen, that's why he was first attracted to George at the pub. George was tall with a beard that had touches of grey. Paolo was George's type; swarthy, compact and he also sported a beard. They dated for about a year-and-a-half and then bought a house together. As the one who made a larger salary, George had a much larger stake in the house and felt Paolo should make up the difference with chores around the house. Paolo wasn't sure this was a fair deal, but if that's what George wanted, he'd go along with it.

He and George moved into the home, and for about twelve years made a good life together. They renovated the old house to give it a modern make-over. They entertained frequently with Paolo doing the heavy lifting when it came to the cleaning up.

Then George started coming home from work and not speaking to Paolo, as if Paulo was invisible. Paolo had no idea what was going on with his partner. After three years of living this way, Paolo initiated a breakup.

They decided that since the house was big enough to accommodate them and was appreciating in the market, Paolo would move into the basement. This arrangement worked with each of them living separate lives.

Then George met Monty online — he was from out of the country and stayed in the house when he visited. After a year of going back and forth between countries, Monty and George got married. Same-sex marriage is recognized in Canada and would help Monty become a landed immigrant and eventually a Canadian citizen.

The newly-weds wanted to buy Paolo out at a 28% share of the house. Paolo had 30% in the house and that's what he wanted back. George and Monty refused.

Paolo went to his lawyer and told him he wanted his 30%. The lawyer informed him he was entitled to 50% of the house, equalization of George's CPP, 50% of the other assets accumulated during their relationship, and possibly support payments. Paolo told George that he wanted his 30 per cent, or he would go for the rest of the booty. George was furious but agreed to the terms.

You're probably thinking that Paola should've gone for everything he could've gotten, but he just wanted what they originally agreed upon. A little fairness goes a long way when you're splitting up. The point is that the shared living arrangement worked well until it didn't.

Paolo ended up with enough funds from his ex's buy-out to purchase an apartment of his own, and that's all he wanted for his own financial security.

CHAPTER 7: If I had a Million Dollars Financial Gurus

It was time for Step 2 in my separation process. I visited our Financial Advisor to see what would be involved in splitting our investments.

Ace and I joined our accounts when we were in our 20s, so this step seemed daunting. Brett could give me a better understanding of where I'd be financially after we split up. I was pretty sure I'd be okay, but I needed to know for sure that the numbers I saw on the statements would translate into a financially secure future after the breakup.

Not everyone has a financial advisor, but you may have an accountant who can go through your accounts with you. (We didn't have an accountant because Ace used to program accounting software and did our taxes for us.)

If you don't have any idea of what your financial picture is, going to your banker is a good first step. Also, getting online access to your accounts is critical for you to know where you stand financially.

Three Stages of Retirement
Brett welcomed me into his modern sleek office. I explained what Ace and I'd gone through since he'd retired.

He looked unsurprised and nonjudgmental, so I felt more at ease. He has about five clients in their 60s go through divorce every year. He said 10,000 people per day in North America retire.

He laid out the stages and concerns of retirement in the first 18 months, as follows:

- 0 to 6 months – Do we have enough to retire on? Who am I?

- 6 to 12 months – It's just the two of us. What do we do next?

- 12 to 18 months – Let's do something: Start a business, buy a franchise, start an Air B&B.

We hadn't made it to the 18-month mark yet and we were in melt-down mode. Brett was sympathetic and said that the first 18 months are the hardest.

> *New retirees are healthier... retire younger. They call me and want $100,000 to bike around the world. They go back to university. There are retirement homes that have shuttle buses to take them to the University of British Columbia, where the tuition is free after 65. It's more expensive to retire now too, because their travel expenses go up and they eat healthier, like groceries from Whole Foods.*

His parents split at the age of 65. His mom went to meditate with the Dalai Lama in Tibet. His dad played golf and smoked cigars. They engaged in a financial battle and Brett became caught in the middle of it all.

The war was over his mother's inheritance from his grandfather. Family law has changed in Canada regarding inheritances. You no longer have to include your inheritance in the marital assets; however, any growth in the inheritance, such as capital appreciation, dividends and interest, is part of joint property. The growth of his mother's inheritance was worth much more than the original inheritance. That interest had to be split 50/50 between his mom and dad. Brett's concerned that if his dad remarries, that half of their inheritance from their grandfather could go to his dad's new wife and eventually to her children, and not to him and his siblings.

I told him this didn't apply to us as our parents were still alive and well at the time, and still are at the time of this writing.

Of course, this could be mitigated if Brett's father gave his children their inheritance before he married or cohabitated with a new partner.

Another option would be for his father to have a pre-nup or *Cohabitation Agreement* and put his intentions in his Will regarding the inheritance from his ex-wife.

Creating a Vision Board Together

Brett said that about half of the people who retire each year, have what is called a "soft landing", just like in an airplane when the pilot is so good you hardly feel the touchdown. The other half, like Ace, have a "hard landing".

Ace was so happy to be retired, so how could he be having a hard landing? Brett said that it sounded like Ace's identity was wrapped up in his job, and that's what was making our marriage suffer.

Ace read lots of books on transitioning into retirement and we'd visited Brett to do our financial planning, but we'd neglected to do any relationship planning.

"I had one couple each create an individual vision board for their retirement," he said. He demonstrated what the vision board looked like by drawing a circle on a piece of paper. He had them write what their vision for their retirement was inside the circle. "Next, I put them side-by-side and compared them," he said. He drew two circles intersecting, like a Venn diagram, and filled them with like items at the intersection. Then they can really start to find common things they want to do together. However, you and your partner could simply write your goals separately, then highlight, the common ones. Or, you could get crafty and make collages on poster-board with images cut from glossy magazines. But a retirement vision word list for Ace and I, would look like this:

CATHALYNN	ACE
Travel	Artificial Intelligence programming
Teach abroad	Play guitar
Become close as a couple	Run
<u>Write books & blog</u>	Mountain bike
Learn to fly	HAM radio club
	Photography club
	<u>Write books & blog</u>
	Join Search and Rescue
	Teach programming

The only thing Ace and I had in common was to write books and blog, which are solitary pursuits that rarely foster our relationship at all.

***

Brett's vision board exercise made me realize that Ace thought of retirement as HIS retirement rather than our retirement, and that was the root of our problem.

***

Ace and I should've talked to Brett about the relationship goals and expectations and what it would take to finance them, because no money = no fun.

For example, staying at home was cost effective but relationship negative for me.

Travelling and having adventures would take more finances but would yield more positive relationship dividends.

Divorce is far more expensive than staying together is, so in the end it's significantly more financially positive. This was a cost balance analysis in language that Ace would understand.

Brett then moved on to what I thought our meeting was purely going to be about when I first walked in, which was a financial checklist of what an over 50s couple typically shares financially, to see what applied to us.

This list will vary depending upon which country you live in:

- Retirement savings plans - Check

- Spousal retirement savings plans- Check

- Tax Free Savings Accounts (TFSAs) - Check

- Registered Education Savings Plans (RESPs) - N/A

- Bonds – N/A

- Collections, such as stamps and coins – N/A

- Safety Deposit Box(es) Contents, such as currency, jewels, precious metals – N/A

- Debts, such as LOCs, credit cards, mortgages – Check

- House - Check

- Recreational Property - N/A

- Investment Property - Check

- Inheritance growth - N/A

- Business - N/A

- Children (minor or adult)—including children with disabilities - N/A

- Ageing parents - Check

Brett pointed out that divorcing couples don't have to go through this process alone, as you can include:

- Accountants – Canadian, American or Foreign depending on your holdings – N/A

- Trustees - In the case of children with disabilities who need trusts put in place – N/A

- Bankers - Who have toolkits to hand out - Check

- Trustees – N/A

- Lawyers - Check

- Counsellors – N/A

Tips for Choosing a Financial Advisor

Your Financial Advisor is responsible for your net worth aside from your real estate holdings.

My friend, Christopher Powell, who was a Financial Advisor, says, "The average person spends more time researching movie ratings than they do their Financial Advisor."

Chris says to pick a financial advisor like you would a dentist, through word-of-mouth, reviews, reputation and online research.

"A legitimate Financial Advisor must provide you with information on investor protection and rights. It's a major red flag if this information isn't provided or available," warns Chris.

A Certified Financial Planner (CFP) designation means that your advisor is qualified to do financial planning.

If the Financial Advisor is trading stocks and mutual funds for you, they will have registration numbers, for example, for the Investment Industry Regulatory Organization of Canada (IIROC) (www.iiroc.ca) and Mutual Fund Dealers Association of Canada (MFDA) (www.mfda.ca), respectively.

You can look up their registration numbers to see if there are any complaints lodged against them.

Brett also gave some tips for picking a financial advisor if you don't already have one:

1. Hire someone as if they were going to be the Chief Financial Officer (CFO) for your family, who will ensure the financial well-being of your family.

2. When you interview them look for someone you can connect with.

3. Ask family and friends for recommendations.

He advised women to get familiar with their financial situation as 75-80% of the women in their 60s that he talks to don't know what's going on with their finances. The husband has always taken care of the money.

In my case, the day-to-day banking fell to me, and we made investment decisions together. Ace and I tried to both know what each other did to run the household. We wanted to be able to manage things in case of illness or worse.

I left Brett's office with confirmation that financially I was going to be okay, even without spousal support. Ace wouldn't have to go back to work, which would make the separation go smoothly.

Also, I left with a better understanding that Ace was lost right now and redefining his identity.

Perhaps, I'd been impatient and wondered if within six months to a year, Ace would find his way back to me.

Financial Hacks

It's likely you will have a lower income and standard of living at least in the short term as a result of your separation.

If you know you're going to leave your partner, it's a good idea to start building a war chest as soon as you know your intentions, especially if you have dependents.

Some of the Dos and Don'ts include:

- DO have your mail go to a PO Box or address that your partner won't be able to access. Be careful not to leave mail with the new address lying around where your partner could see it.

- DO save money that is legitimately yours in an account in your name only.

- DO get your own credit card.

- DO close out joint credit accounts.

- DON'T clean out your joint accounts.

- DON'T incur any debts.

- DON'T make any significant purchases, like a new car, house, or recreational items.

- DON'T make any career changes that will lower your income or put you at risk to lose your job.

Chris recommends:

Before you make the move, ask your bank to hold (block withdrawals) from all joint credit accounts.

I have heard more than once of a breakup where one partner takes it upon themselves to empty the accounts. If you have a line of credit, or a joint credit card, ask the bank to stop withdrawals — "place a hold on the account."

Do not be tempted to take money yourself. No matter how entitled you may feel to it, it can only hurt you during the divorce and will appear malicious.

When it comes to your savings and chequing accounts, which are joint, transfer what is rightfully yours (not what you FEEL entitled to) to an account in your name only.

Keep a record of each transaction and evidence that the money is indeed yours, especially if the funds are a substantial portion of your joint liquid assets.

Again, you do not want to appear malicious and leave your partner with nothing. This will not look good in court. Even though you put a hold on the account, your partner can still go in there and ask them to remove that hold and they will, so this is very temporary.

The best course of action is to get into the bank together if at all possible – ASAP. Ditto for joint investment accounts - you may wish to visit your advisor very early in the process, as it can take up to five weeks to transfer the funds if you choose to change Financial Advisors.

Chris cautions that you're responsible for half of your partner's debt, including mortgage and lines of credit, which is the reason for putting holds on the joint credit accounts and credit cards.

He says that with e-transfer you don't really need to have anything joint with your partner at all. For example, you can e-transfer each other for rent or mortgage, car, and other payments.

However, with relationships amongst the 50-plus demographic it's quite common to have everything joint, especially things like spousal retirement plans for tax benefits.

Also, you may reduce banking and investment fees by having fewer accounts as well.

Some couples have separate accounts and one joint account to contribute to for household bills. But these inconveniences and fees may be worth it in the long run, if the relationship blows up. Unfortunately, we don't know how our partner will react in a breakup when we commit to them.

Exercise 10. Trying on Solutions for Size

Suggest-propose some mutual relationship goals to your partner to discuss and prioritize so that you can work together towards building a stronger relationship.

My next step was to talk to real estate agents about what to do about our properties. The markets were good, so that wasn't a worry. Although, it always seems more difficult to buy than sell. We'll look at this in detail in the next chapter.

CHAPTER 8: Our House
Real Estate on the Front Lines

Step 3 in my separation process was to know what to do about our properties.

I thought that we would likely sell our marital home and the one-room condo. I'd want a larger space than the current shoe-box sized condo to live in full-time in the city and Ace would want a smaller home wherever he ultimately ended up living.

It seemed pre-emptive to contact a real estate agent, but I wanted to know how other couples fared once they split up, regarding their real estate options.

After all, the marital home is on the frontline of the breakup.

At least one of the homes we've purchased was on the market because of divorce. Obviously, this information is kept hush-hush, so that the seller still gets the optimal price for their home.

***

FAQ - What will happen to my house?

Usually, the jointly owned home is sold. When the home is sold both parties divide up any profit left after the mortgage and fees are paid or split the debt and go their separate ways.

However, in Canada, if the house belonged to you before the relationship it will continue to belong to you.

The same applies if the house belonged to your partner and they brought the house into the relationship, then it remains theirs after the split.

If your name is on the title then half, or whatever portion was agreed upon between the two of you, belongs to you and you have the legal right to live there.

Even if your partner changes the locks on your home, you can call a locksmith and legally regain entry to your home. If you're afraid for your safety, call the police first for advice.

If only one of you has your name on the title, you may need a lawyer's help to sort out division of property. You and your partner are likely entitled to half the house.

You or partner may decide to buy the other out, but that takes a lot of capital so usually the house will be sold.

The decision about what to do with the house will be outlined in the *Separation Agreement*, or settled in mediation, arbitration, or divorce court if you can't come to an agreement.

***

For privacy reasons, there are no statistics in Canada for home sales based on age or reason for sale either by the member-based Canada Real Estate Board (CREA) or their local branches. Neither does the Canada Mortgage and Housing Corporation (CMHC), or the Canadian Bankers Association track this kind of information, so it's difficult to know just how the real estate market is impacted by separation and divorce.

In the UK they track the reason for home sales as evident in James Pickford's article *Divorce: Dividing Up the Family Home.*

He quotes a researcher, Lucian Cook from the Savills estate agency. Cook "found the total housing equity held by over-50s on divorce rocketed from £4.5bn to £8.29bn over 15 years — a rise of 84 per cent."

In Australia, there's also a trend of increased house sales due to divorce. In Williams article, *Divorce-led property sales on the rise amid recent downturn,* experts say, "Total property resales of 276,800 per year or about 18 divorces for every 100 residential resales." The article states that, "The median age at divorce for both men and women … is 45.5 years for men and 42.9 years for women, with the median duration of a marriage at 12 years."

Overall, the agents I talked to noticed a trend that the seeds of grey divorce began in their clients who were in their 40s, not in their 50s. A real estate agent on the Sunshine Coast of BC says that the last three showings he had were all sales due to divorce, although not necessarily grey divorce.

The agent said that while most couples wait until the children leave home to split up, some spouses may live separately within the home. For example, the father may move to the basement and the kids are none the wiser.

When couples sell their marital homes, an agent I interviewed said it's rare that they don't get back into the market again, but in an area that is more affordable.

The oldest couple he's seen separated were in their 80s after more than four decades of marriage, and it was initiated by the wife. However, there is a happy ending to the story as they are now in the same retirement home and it's bringing them back together again.

He often sees the wife's family, stepping in and helping her with the family, as does another agent in the same area. He's seen daughters move onto the parents' property, if not into their home, while the husbands end up renting or buying somewhere else.

An agent in a suburb of the lower mainland of Vancouver has seen at least three couples in their 60s divorce due to infidelity. She says that the husband is the one who leaves the community, whereas the wife stays, because it's where her adult children and grandchildren are based. She's seen spouses evade divorce by dodging court dates.

An agent in the sky-high priced area of West Vancouver, Lauren, agrees that divorce has shifted to the 40s when women are still having children. She finds men are "trading in their wives for younger models while keeping their ex-wives on tight financial leashes in the marital home without the support and ability to maintain it. The burdens are laid on the female, while the males move on without stress."

She says that economics drives the decisions when it comes to divorce. Both parties may have to leave the area after selling their home as there may not be much money left after paying out the mortgage, commission, deferred property taxes, lawyers, moving costs, and so on. They may even need to move to another province to find something affordable to buy or rent.

Lauren finds that women have to consider how much they will get per month before they know what they will be able afford for housing post-separation and divorce, especially if they have an angry spouse. They may find themselves living on a shoestring if the ex is "visceral and vindictive."

Furthermore, she said, "Over time the ex-husband feels less obligated to do the right thing," when it comes to support payments.

She says, "If you can't afford to get a formal agreement and don't have your own money, you are left at a disadvantage."

There are strict criteria for eligibility for legal aid, but it doesn't hurt to apply. All the countries addressed in this book have legal aid information available for Canada, the US, the UK, Australia and New Zealand. Please go to the Author's book website:

breakupmakeuporshakeup.wordpress.com

In Canada, a Duty Counsel is another option. It's not ideal because the lawyer could have 50 cases on the go, but it's better than no counsel at all.

There are also non-profit organizations, such as the Vancouver and Lower Mainland Multicultural Family Support Service Society (www.vlmfss.ca).

However, without their own income and enough funds for a legal retainer for a good lawyer, women are at the mercy of their exes.

Looking at a more stable and affordable market, an agent in Ottawa, Ontario said couples can divide the profits from the sale of their home and still afford to each purchase a home.

The agent said the oldest couple he saw split up were in their 70s. The trend he sees is that when older couples split, they tend to go into rentals or care homes.

The worst way to announce a divorce that he's seen was a wife announcing she was leaving her long-time spouse in front of all their friends and family at a New Year's party at midnight — surprise!

As one Financial Advisor told me, "If you want to double your money, get married. If you want to halve your money, get divorced."

This advisor also shares an example of a couple who are splitting in their mid-forties with a huge mortgage and young children.

In the case of this mid-40s couple, he notes, they are splitting debt rather than assets and will likely never recover.

CHAPTER 9: Shirley's Story: The Sweet Escape

Just like you need a plan for evacuating your house when it's burning down, it's smart to have an escape plan if you're planning to leave your partner or get them to leave.

The following is an escape plan that I helped devise with my friend, Shirley.

Our neighbour Shirley was having the worst time of her life. Her boyfriend was draining their bank account with spending money drinking in bars, and flying and maintaining his small airplane.

If that wasn't bad enough, he was cheating on her in a public way with one of his coworkers.

Her boyfriend stayed with Shirley a few nights a week, but disappeared for days at a time staying with his lover.

Then, he'd come back, drunk and coerce her into sex. She was terrified of him but didn't have the nerve to call the police.

Shirley came to me one afternoon in tears and trembling. She told me that she was afraid he would rape her next time he came home drunk.

She needed to get her abusive partner out of the house but didn't know what to do.

I outlined a plan wherein she could keep the house and get rid of him permanently

First of all, she made a call and had her teenage daughter extend her stay with a friend until this domestic situation could be sorted.

We went back to Shirley's house and helped her move all of his s**t out of the house into boxes and piled it up in the carport.

Shirley had a locksmith change the locks.

She stayed with us at night after work, because she didn't know when he would return.

Shirley also turned off her cell phone every night.

When he came back a few nights later from being with his mistress, he found all his things packed up in the carport and his house key didn't work.

He banged on the doors and windows of the house all night. At least she didn't have to live through a night of terror.

He picked up his boxes, packed them in his truck, and moved in with his new girlfriend. Shirley was free of him and the threat of abuse and rape.

Shirley managed to buy him out of his share of the house and stay where she was. Her daughter still had a couple years of high-school left to finish, so it was important to her to give her a stable home to live in.

I was relieved that the plan actually worked.

His name was on the title, so he could have broken a window and let himself in, but we counted on him not knowing his rights and it worked.

Most importantly, she had an escape plan.

If you're in an abusive relationship, make a plan and practice how you will get out safely. If you are being abused, call the police if it's an emergency. See Chapter 22 for further details on dealing with violence-abuse and Emergency, Transition and Safe homes.

Shirley was in a dangerous situation that could escalated quickly. Breakups are when partners are at most risk.

What Shirley did right to protect herself was to tell us she needed help.

If she didn't have friends, she could've gone to the police for assistance to have him removed from the home. I was really proud of her for taking care of herself.

It was difficult for the next few months.

Shirley was let go from her secretarial job. She got a sales job but wasn't ready to deal with the public and was fired.

Shirley then took classes on interior design that she really enjoyed. She eventually found a new position. More exciting, her dream of becoming a grandmother came true. We lost touch with each other. A mutual friend told me that Shirley passed away from cancer. She was confused at the end from the pain medications but she was surrounded by her family.

Coming up next chapter: *Hannah's Story: He Can't Hurt me Ever Again.*

CHAPTER 10: Hannah's Story: Big Girls Don't Cry
He Can't Hurt Me Ever Again

Hannah, like Shirley, came up with a plan to keep her home. She managed to get her abusive spouse to leave the marital home.

Her plan was wise because of the following:

She was outside of the house.

She waited until her partner was out of the house to get everything ready.

She alerted the police of her plan.

She had a neighbour keep watch for her partner.

Both of the partners wanted to stay in the marital home, but she needed to stay and raise her children. Her abusive husband needed to leave, so she needed a careful plan that took many years to execute.

Hannah was a young vulnerable girl, who had to grow up fast. She was bored and unchallenged in high-school, so she dropped out in Grade 10.

Hannah left home the first week of October 1978 to live with one of her sisters in Vancouver, not far from her parents' home, for six months.

After living with her sister and working at a restaurant, Hannah found a job at a lumberyard where she first met Ted.

Hannah moved back to her parents' home where Ted worked on the military base.

They dated for about seven months, then:

Ted and the guys in his unit had to stay after work for their monthly Personnel Reports (PRs). We ended up having to wait in his car right up until about 10:30 pm before he was called in. Ted made reservations at the swankiest restaurant in town and made arrangements to have my engagement ring put in my dessert.

He grabbed a case of beer to bring with us to the lake for after dinner to celebrate. As we sat in the car in the parking lot waiting, he got more and more angry. The angrier he got, the more he drank.

When he was called into the office to have his face-to-face with the Captain, he had about three-quarters of the case of beer and then made the mistake of telling the Captain exactly what he thought of his month-end PR.

When the Captain stood up abruptly and reached to take Ted's hat off, Ted thought he was taking a swipe at him and punched him. The MPs took him to the drunk tank.

After spending the weekend in jail, the ring he'd left to be put in my dessert was gone. The restaurant refused to pay him anything to replace it. I received a cheap version of it in silver with Hungarian crystals. He got down on one knee in the sand in his dress uniform and asked me to marry him, and I said yes.

Ted's assault on his Captain was dealt with swiftly, and within the week he was given a choice, Hannah said, "To voluntarily quit the military with an honourable discharge, or go to court martial, more than likely end up going to jail, and end up with a dishonourable discharge." He chose to quit.

He waited until AFTER I said I'd marry him to tell me that he was quitting the army and going back east to Ontario. If I had known that he was quitting the army, I probably would have said NO.

What I didn't know until I got there was that his family was on welfare. Ted's buy-out from the military would have been able to support us on our own, but as soon as he got it, he gave it to his dad.

Hannah found a full-time job at a security company.

My paycheck put gas in our car, a gas-guzzling '73 Toronado, and the rest he gave to his parents to assist with bills but it was usually spent on booze for his dad and him.

Our wedding ceremony was pretty but not fancy, short, and had about 20 people in attendance.

While we were on the last day of our honeymoon, I became violently sick. I remember barely making it to the bathroom toilet in time. We checked out of our room and went straight to the hospital to get checked, as it was between the motel and home. I was asked to do the pee in the bottle thing. I was pregnant.

We were elated, excited, and quite happy with this announcement and couldn't wait to share it with everyone.

Ted first began to abuse her while she was pregnant with their first child, Hannah recalls:

When I was six months preggo, I was in the kitchen talking to his mom about dinner; she was stirring hamburger in the pan. I was ironing clothes across from her in the big country-style kitchen. The men were in the living room watching TV, and the rest of the family were not in attendance.

His mother was being sympathetic because the smell of raw hamburger made me nauseous, and we were joking about it because I usually ended up in the bathroom, puking.

Ted apparently was eavesdropping and misheard our conversation and thought I was being derogatory and telling her she was a lousy cook.

He came out into the kitchen enraged and punched me in the face. She immediately ran over and whopped him on the head with the hot frying pan with the burger in it and knocked his ass out.

After a year in this dysfunctional household, they moved to Winnipeg where Ted got a job with the railway. Hannah had enough of his drinking and chronic unemployment.

Ted worked only four years in the 15-and-a-half years I stuck it out with him.

I was still being abused by him. He constantly kept me from normal things, he even cut up my driver's license so I couldn't drive, chose my friends for me, did not let me out of the house, etc.

He told me almost every day, that if I left I was not going to be taking "his" kids and that if he couldn't have me, no one else would.

I called the local Royal Canadian Mounted Police (RCMP) to let them know I was leaving him and that he may become extremely violent.

I also asked my next-door neighbour for help, in case this occurred. The neighbour kept an eye out for me in order to call the cops in case he did get violent.

When Ted came home… I had his bags packed and on the front step. I was sitting on it out in the open.

I knew there was a chance he wouldn't beat me in public. Instead, he got angry, yelled, went upstairs, had a shower, came downstairs, picked up the coffee table and threw it through the big living-room window out onto the lawn, grabbed the two suitcases and left, driving off tires squealing and making death threats as he went.

The landlord came an hour later and changed the locks.

I went into hiding with the new Victim Services Program run by the RCMP.

I never went back to Ted. I found out later most people who are abused go back to their abuser.

I might have been naive and terrified, but I was not stupid! Damned if I'd go back once I took the first step.

Hannah's ex stalked her. She describes the terrifying ordeal:

He stalked me with weapons in the car, he bought a police scanner so he would know when I'd called the cops on him and would disappear before they showed up.

Ted constantly followed me, made threats, or begged for me to take him back for three years.

He broke into my house twice that first year and raped me. I was never able to get a peace bond against him because there was no proof that he was stalking me.

There is one piece of technology that wasn't available to Hannah at the time but may help someone in this situation now — Wi-Fi-enabled home monitoring cameras that make it easier to catch intruders.

For example, PetCube, www.petcube.com), is motion-activated so you can watch it live (or later) and see who has come and gone from your house for free. Plus, you can use the microphone to scare them off remotely.

Motion sensitive cameras can be used both indoors and outdoors to send alerts.

The advantage is these feeds go to a central server in the Cloud, so you don't need a computer to store the data.

The intruder can destroy your computer and you won't lose any incriminating video evidence needed to prosecute or get restraining orders.

Hannah wanted to divorce Ted, but he didn't agree and made it impossible. She recalls:

The first two times, he told the system that we could work it out, so the divorce was not approved. The next seven times I tried to divorce him, over the span of 20 years or so, he would get the call from the bailiff that they were coming to serve him documents and he would move. To the tune of about $3500- $4500 per attempt. I gave up.

Hannah has done her best to move forward with her own life, "I have had four relationships during the past 23 years and left all of them at the first signs of possible verbal abuse. I left as fast and as far as I possibly could."

After nearly 25 years she received a phone call:

"I received a phone call from a lawyer in Alberta. They said that Ted would like to file for a divorce from me. I was so excited. I'm counting the days that I receive that little piece of paper that says I am now divorced. He can no longer hurt me, inside or out."

Mothers like Hannah in abusive unbalanced relationships work even harder than other mothers to give their children what they need, like a roof over their heads.

These mothers are judged for not leaving the dysfunctional relationship, yet when they do leave they are judged for leaving. How can they win?

Lulu's situation echoes Hannah's story on many levels. Lulu and her children never knew whether or not they would have a home of their own.

CHAPTER 11: Lulu's Story: Leaving You

Four generations live under Lulu's roof: her mother, her daughter, Ellen, and Ellen's husband and son.

Lulu is an elegant woman, who's always dressed in fashionable outfits, sporting statement piece jewelry, square thin-framed glasses and silver hair stylishly cut by her daughter-in-law, a top hair stylist.

She was only 20, living in a small town in Saskatchewan and on the rebound, when she agreed to marry Gene, a somber Mennonite man, after only six weeks of acquaintance. On that April day in 1971, Lulu knew it was a mistake as soon as she walked down the aisle.

"I wish someone had whispered to me that it was okay to back out," she said.

Shortly into the marriage, she confided to the Lutheran minister who married them that she'd made a mistake and had to get out of the marriage. He acknowledged that she was right, but she didn't have the chance to bring it up with Gene. His father was suddenly ill with his first bout of cancer. Gene lost his mother just before they married.

The young couple helped with the old man's care and he recovered. Lulu worked at the family fabric store.

Gene found work locally after going back to school for a few years.

However, her father-in-law wanted them to move out of their apartment and get a home of their own, so they could care for Gene's 12-year old sister after her father-in-law died when his cancer returned.

They bought a house with a pool and a Lincoln Town car. Gene bought out a scrap metal business.

Lulu didn't want to start a family of their own so she used birth control but she still got pregnant. Around that time, Gene's health began to suffer — he lost his hair, dropped a significant amount of weight off of his 6' 4" frame, and developed environmental allergies.

Then things started to go downhill with the scrap business. They lost everything and moved in with Lulu's parents in a different town. Gene sold insurance and Lulu, who was pregnant again, managed a women's clothing store. Two more children were to follow, all resulting from birth control fails.

Unfortunately, Gene lost his job at the insurance company when their youngest was still little. He moved to Moose Jaw to manage a company. Lulu and the children later followed him.

In her 40s, Lulu, went back to university through night-school. Lulu was excited to be at university and got a job before she graduated.

Gene was jealous of Lulu being around the professors and men in the adult education program. When he was drunk, he pushed her into walls pinning her there.

Then came news that Gene was let go. The family lived off of her student loan and his Employment Insurance

(EI). Gene did the odd carpentry job, but mostly stayed in the garage working on his own projects.

Lulu said, "When you're always in survival mode, you have to put your happiness, your marriage on the backburner. That's a luxury on Maslow's scale that you're not allowed. Your children want a normal life; they do not want your drama." Maslow's Hierarchy of Needs is represented by a triangle with the bottom third (the base) addressing basic physiological and safety needs, the middle third of the triangle addressing psychological needs, and the small top third of the triangle addressing needs for self-fulfillment.

Lulu comments, "He couldn't get taking care of us down, so he tried to be authoritarian." She was trapped in a loveless marriage with a man who was neither provider nor protector.

Her parents bought a house for her in Moose Jaw. Gene left for Alberta to stay with his family. Lulu was pleased to be separated from Gene, but after five months he came back. Lulu took him back out of pity. But it didn't last long, and he went back to his family in Alberta.

She moved back to her parents' home to save money and rented out the Moose Jaw house. Gene moved on and even had a new girlfriend. However, he moved to Regina to be closer to his children and wanted to reconcile with Lulu. She took him back because now she had adolescent boys to raise and needed his help. They moved back to Moose Jaw and she got a job in her field.

At the same time, her oldest daughter was newly divorced and moving to Vancouver to be with the new man in her life. Lulu helped her move her things to the Pacific Coast.

When Lulu was in Vancouver helping her daughter with the move, she met up with a girlfriend who was dating a nice man. This friend turned out to be instrumental in changing Lulu's life.

When Lulu returned to Moose Jaw, Gene told her that he and the boys wanted to start a business together. Although Lulu had her reservations, she financed it by putting a second mortgage on the house that her parents had given to her.

One day the phone rang, and it was from her friend in Vancouver, "I'm moving in with my man and my apartment is going to come up, but if you want it you can have it." A week later, her friend called her back.

"So, Lulu, do you want my apartment?" she asked.

"Yes, I do." Lulu hung up and told Gene she was leaving at the end of the month.

"I had to leave him," she tells me, "because he was never going to leave the house." She packed up her things.

Unfortunately, the manufacturing company that Gene and the boys started quickly went bust. As a result, she lost the home that her parents gave her.

Lulu moved to Vancouver. It took nine months for her to find work there.

Gene developed cancer and came out west for a visit. He returned to Moose Jaw. When he became terminal, Lulu and her three children were all living on the West Coast at that time, but all of them went back when he was hospitalized to be at his side when he passed.

***

Lulu and I wrap up our conversation and her youngest child, Maya, who lives in a wing of this generous home joins us in the spacious living-room that was filled with afternoon sunlight.

"In what way do you think your parents' relationship might have affected your choices in relationships?" I ask this sphinx-like woman in her early 30s, with short auburn hair, and an elegant script tattoo—*Love*—peeking out from the sleeve on her left arm. Her head turns and brown-golden eyes look hypnotically into mine.

"I dated every kind of toxic man out there: alcoholic, cocaine-snorting, drug addicted, you name it. I was a beacon in the night for every man with mental illness, until I met my husband," she said.

Lulu said she dated each needy man for a year or two, "mothering and smothering" them, while letting them emotionally abuse her. She learned from her parents the following:

- To never have unprotected sex and get tied down with children.

- Learn to compromise.

- Try not to do everything yourself.

- Don't be the one to wear the pants.

- Don't be married to someone like my father.

- Do everything united.

- Fight fair.

Maya models her happy relationship with her husband after the loving healthy relationship her grandparents had. She saw the marital break-down of her parents at its worst. She was in her last semester of high-school when Lulu left for the West Coast, and stayed with her father, Gene, until she graduated.

Her dad was relieved of the guilt of his family's expectations and was happier. As soon as she graduated, she moved west to be with her mom and siblings.

Lulu's oldest daughter, Beatrice, is a 42-year-old mother of two energetic young ladies. She never imagined herself to be a single, unemployed mom of two kids from two different relationships. Her first marriage was at 21; she divorced at 26 and has been single for the past two years at 42.

"Why don't you leave, Mom?" Beatrice remembers pleading with her mother, as did her siblings.

Beatrice lacked self-love and not have a good sense of her own self-worth. She never chose partners. She let them choose her whether she liked them or not.

She is happier on her own, busy raising her girls and starting a new business.

She concludes with these thoughts:

> *I became a leaver in my relationships. I would not stay like my mom had. So, I attracted and accepted men into my life that I knew deep down were temporary.*

> *Now my goal is to hold my standards high enough and to actively choose someone I genuinely love,*

someone who is willing and able to be there for the long haul, for both me and my girls.

My challenge as a mother to two little girls is to show them the middle path through all of our experiences. To show them that they are enough as they are. To really know true self love. I want them to believe they are worthy of great love and to truly feel that before committing to anyone.

As a take-away for readers she says:

- *Get to a place in your life that you know deep in your bones that you're enough as you are.*

- *Have a very clear vision of the life you want to live and have high standards for yourself.*

- *Listen to your gut—if you are feeling something in your body that is a warning, heed it.*

- *Take your time to get all the information you need; there is no need to rush into relationships.*

- *Make no decisions out of fear.*

- *No one is perfect and you need to create your own fairytale.*

- *Forgive yourself and others; relationships are only mirrors of where we are in our relationship to self.*

Lulu's escape from a bad marriage was protracted, but she did the best she could in her tragic situation in the time and environment that provided absolutely no support to women.

Due to Lulu's persistence, she escaped her partner and is happily immersed in family life as the matriarch.

However, she did end up losing her main asset of the family home to her estranged husband's failed business. She also lost her job just before retirement. She will continue to be a renter for the rest of her life, but she did find a way to escape her controlling partner by moving far away from him.

In that long journey of marriage, anything can happen to change our partner's health. There are bumps along the road that can plunge our partner into a depression, or as the pandemic demonstrated that none of us are beyond human frailty, especially as we age.

Heart attack, stroke and dementia can rob us of growing old together, as you'll see in my friend Linda's story. Linda's been extremely savvy about real estate even if she's spent some time house-sitting and renting to keep distanced from her physically abusive husband.

CHAPTER 12: Linda's Story: Run Runaway

Linda brushes a lock of her black hair shot with silver out of her eyes.

"Tell me how you met him," I ask this petite dynamo as we have a coffee at a popular local cafe.

> *It was spring on campus and the cherry blossoms were in bloom. We had immediate chemistry. We got married when I was 21. He worked as a teacher and so did I. He became an administrator of a school.*
>
> *When Harvey was 57 he retired, and we managed an inn and the grounds surrounding it in an isolated place for five years. I wanted to leave because it was too isolated, so we bought a house on the Sunshine Coast.*
>
> *A year later, Harvey was on the floor when I came home. They helicoptered him to Vancouver, but it was too late to give him the clot-busting drugs because they didn't know how long he'd been lying on the floor.*
>
> *Because Harvey was fit and young in his early 60s, he made a phenomenal recovery, but deficits began to appear. I'd lost my husband. He lost his motivation to do anything. He was depressed and didn't comply with taking medicine or following doctor's orders.*

He was angry to the point of rage and fearful. I lived in fear of his violence, and he wasn't taking care of himself.

My husband pushed me up against the wall with his arm pinned on my throat. He also had no fear of pushing or punching me in public. Once he punched me in the arm, while I was in the car at the ferry terminal.

After that outburst of violence, she went to see a lawyer.

I was prepared to write a Separation Agreement. She advised me to leave him or kick him out and start documenting everything. She also said that since I was in charge of all the finances, I didn't need to do anything else but physically separate.

One day during one of Harvey's rages, I locked myself in the bathroom. I'd already put a packed bag in the car. I made a break for the car.

I spent three or four months teaching in Mexico, and I didn't want to come home. I'd flit in and out briefly at home. I did this for three or four years before I found a rental place on the Sunshine Coast again.

I went to a horse healing retreat called Run with the Herd, where we got Reiki treatments under these tents and the horses would go freely among us.

I was meditating on the first day, and a black stallion, Magic, lay down beside me and put his head in my lap. I stroked him. When I was on the Reiki table, he put his muzzle on my heart and breathed in and out, healing my broken heart.

Harvey and I saw each other at family events and were civil. Despite me telling family and friends about Harvey's abuse towards me, they didn't believe me.

Around Christmas he got the flu and looked frail. This is common for people who've had a traumatic brain injury.

I wanted to move into the ground floor of the townhouse that I'd picked out for Harvey to live in. I was tired of living in a rental suite. I told Harvey that I wanted to renovate the lower level as a suite for myself. If he didn't like it, we'd get a divorce and I'd move him out.

He wanted me back as his wife and I wasn't interested, but I did want to move closer to the main part of town. He accepted my terms. The reno is going great.

I plan to put a lock on the door; and if things don't work out, I'll divorce him and move him out. I don't plan to take care of him but will facilitate his care.

We've been married for 50 years now, even though we're separated. Harvey knocked on my bedroom door the other morning and handed me a rose.

What I'd advise others going through this journey to do is the following:

Breathe.

Get legal advice.

Get your finances in order. Your standard of living may go down, so you need to plan.

Find a good friend to lean on.

Don't be afraid.

Be grateful for your own courage.

People you counted on before may leave, but others will fill that gap.

Don't fear condemnation by your family and children. First, there will be a wall, then a window, a veil, then an open door.

Be independent.

Life changes. Change with it or stagnate.

Linda had the courage to get out of a physically abusive relationship, despite what her family and friends said to the contrary. Harvey managed to hide his rages around other people. She built strong boundaries and practiced self-care by travelling, going on retreats, and maintaining a supportive circle of friends.

She took financial control over the relationship when her partner was incapable of taking care of himself. Linda's strength was to be able to care for her sick husband, be kind, and when her physical and emotional health were threatened, to leave and take care of herself.

She also found a way to have her own home where she wanted it and not be forced out of home ownership by her estranged husband.

Last year, Linda went through chemo and radiation for an aggressive blood cancer. She still lives in a suite in the same building as her estranged husband. She's managing the difficult isolation of the Covid pandemic with her characteristic good cheer and optimism.

Go-bag

Prior to leaving her husband when she had to run for her life, Linda put a go-bag in her trunk for when she had to make an escape.

Doesn't it make sense when you are in a situation of potential danger to have a plan and a drill for how to get out of that situation?

If you have the time to prepare to separate from your abusive partner, wouldn't it make sense to plan where you will go and have a go-bag ready, just like you would for an earthquake, or other disaster? A bag with all your essential documentation you'd need for the lawyer, food, water, clothing, belongings, medications, emergency cash, credit cards, debit cards, cheques, cell phone and charger, electronics, pet food (if applicable) can make all the difference. Camping supplies wouldn't hurt either. Keep the bag stashed in your vehicle, if possible, or hidden elsewhere.

Decide when you will go, when your partner isn't home, if at all possible. Know where you will go.

See *Chapter 22: Emergency, Transition, & Safe Homes* - for emergency numbers, help lines, how to find shelters and other ways to find help lines for Canada, the US, the UK, Australia, and New Zealand.

Make sure you have everything that you need, before you leave even if you're only moving into the basement, hotel or campground, until you can figure things out.

Review again the sample intake form for a lawyer's office that we discussed earlier – there's a lot of information that you'll need when creating a Separation Agreement.

It's likely easier before you walk out, to check that you have everything you need to fill out that form and other separation and divorce forms, including your:

- Marriage license.

- Social Insurance Number/Social Security Number for yourself, your partner, and minor children (if applicable).

- Passports, visas (if applicable).

- Divorce decrees from previous divorces (if applicable).

- Agreements, such as pre- or post-nuptials, cohabitation, or marriage.

- Judgements or pleas.

- Financial records, such as personal and business income tax returns, tax forms, pension forms, bank and investment records for the last five years.

- Employment records for both of you, such as pay stubs for the past year, benefits cards and information, stock options, profit-sharing, travel benefits, expense accounts, discount stock purchase plans, automobile leases and allowances, frequent flyer miles, sick pay, worker's comp, bonuses, military and veteran's benefits, employer contributions to registered savings plans, insurance.

- Income records, business ledgers, casino or lottery winnings, royalties, rental income, sales of property and goods.

- Loan applications made in the last five years.

- Investment records.

- Wills and Trust Agreements, Powers of Attorney, Advanced Health Directives, guardianship papers, and adoption papers.

- Real estate information, such as property tax statements, bills of sale, titles, mortgage papers, and strata agreement.

- Proof of ownership of personal property, such as invoices and insurance on items owned either jointly prior to the relationship or gifted, inherited or purchased during the relationship with a high value, such as jewellery, precious metals, antiques, art or equipment.

- Motor vehicle information, such as lease or loan agreements, bills of sale and titles to all motor vehicles, such as cars, RVs, boats and ATVs.

- Membership cards, documents and statements for clubs, like country clubs, gyms, spas, associations, or organizations.

- A list of safety deposit boxes, their locations and a list or photo of contents.

- Family photos that belong to you.

CHAPTER 13 – Jane's Story: What have We Become?

My friend Jane is the longest-lived friendship among my treasure chest of friends. It was astounding to watch her rise from the scorched earth of her divorce and start over in her 50s.

Jane and her husband, Arnie, met at university where she was doing her law degree and he was studying criminology.

Upon graduation and completion of her articleship, Jane, a sprightly red-head, landed a job in a successful law firm. Slender, dark-haired Arnie worked in law enforcement.

They were thrilled to have a baby girl, Mary. Eventually, Arnie got accepted into the Royal Canadian Mounted Police (RCMP) program in Saskatchewan. Arnie's first posting after graduation was in a small, rural northern town. Jane blogged this about the first posting, that would rip her away from her career and family.

January 2016

ANGER

I wrote that title last July but did not write anything. I am dealing with feelings of anger over exactly what the choices I made for Arnie did to my life. What they 'cost' me. By cost I mean soooo many things. Let me count the ways.

The first cost was — our marriage because his commitment to the RCMP was greater than his commitment to our vows.

Another big cost was being eight hours and 850 kilometres from my mom during 5 out of the last 7 of her years on this planet.

My career was another casualty of the Red Wave that swept the coastline of my life and [reshaped] it. So many things were dragged out to sea. One that has clearly sunk to the bottom of the ocean is my career as a lawyer. There are times I truly ACHE to be the one heading to the courtroom.

Enmeshed with the loss of my career is the loss of a higher income and some semblance of financial security. I will likely be working 'til I die. Had we not left the city, I would have started at the Legal Aid office at a salary higher than anything I had earned, and by now, I would likely be running the family law office. I could give Mary so much more — opportunities, experiences, tools to build her talents.

So many friendships I have pretty much lost count of the people who were part of our world in the city. My health... the time I spent... drained something out of me — something that I can't really name.

The costs pile up, but there are also the things I GOT that I truly do not really want. 20 years of memories, and no one who shares them. A giant bag of guilt — over the hurt I have caused Arnie and Mary and many other people.

As I feel the anger bubble up inside me, I realize I need to write it out. Put it down on paper, or I will surely burst one day and create a different kind of damage. Right around the time of the divorce the movie "The Upside of Anger" came out. While it may not be a classic cinema, there is a quote from it about anger:

"Anger and resentment can stop you in your tracks. The only upside to anger, then is the person you become. And so, I ask the question: who have I become?"

Arnie was excited by his first posting, despite his wife's distress about moving so far away from her family, friends, and career. What about her dream about being a family lawyer?

After five years, Arnie was posted much closer to where Jane's mother lived, so things were looking up for the couple — until they weren't. He broke the news to Jane that he wasn't attracted to her or in love with her anymore and wanted a divorce. She offered to undergo cosmetic procedures and lose weight. She told him to do whatever he wanted even if it meant an affair, but don't leave her.

She drove to her mother's home to tell her the news that her husband was calling it quits, to find her mother still and lifeless on the couch. She went to her mother's side, picked up her cold pale hand and said, "Oh, Mom."

After her mother's funeral, Jane moved in with a friend temporarily so that Mary could stay in the marital home while she and Arnie took turns parenting. Jane found a new position in a small city nearby and bought a home for her and Mary.

With his shift work, Arnie wasn't always able to pick up Mary on his scheduled days. She got accustomed to her dad not being reliable.

Arnie remarried and between the three of them they did a great job of co-parenting Mary. Jane held herself to a high standard and never spoke ill of Arnie in front of Mary.

Jane was so busy with work and parenting she didn't think of dating for a long time. She told me she'd never marry again, but had started to look into online dating. She went on some casual dates and started to have fun.

Then she met Neil.

Tentatively, she let Neil into her life, then they found a home together. After a year of living together, Neil proposed to her and she said yes. They got married and had a honeymoon.

Jane's lessons from her first marriage she brought into her new marriage are, "Don't give up your life for a relationship. And, forgive everyone for everything all the time."

What makes her happy now besides her daughter's well-being?

"Good music, great books, warm weather, finding myself in a 'Holy Instant', where time disappears, and I feel is the LOVE of the Universe. Just remember — our life paths are crooked and winding to help us out how to simply LOVE, because that is all there really is."

They bought a charming home together with room enough for Neil's music studio in the basement and a sewing room for Jane upstairs.

Jane went through a few years of major empty nest blues when her daughter left to live on campus. She also went through ups and downs with jobs but she rolled with it. The key to restoring harmony was to create a home office for Jane where she could conduct online video meetings, as well as her other work tasks and not be disturbed.

Then, COVID-19 found the couple pushed to their limits with both working from home and finding it difficult to spend all their time together, 24-7.

***

I thought about what Jane said about forgiveness and immediately got on a video chat with Ace.

"I don't know if you need to hear this, but for everything that's happened, I forgive you," I said.

"Thank you," he said and beamed. Wow! He did need to hear that. There are primers on the benefits of forgiveness to your mental and physical health at the following links:

- www.psychologytoday.com/ca/basics/forgiveness

- www.mayoclinic.org/healthy-lifestyle/adult-health

Exercise 11. Forgiveness
Write down if you choose to forgive your soon to be ex for their behaviour, even if you don't share it with them.

In the next chapter, we'll look at ways couples approach a reconciliation. In some countries, courts can order couples to seek counseling and attempt reconciliation.

CHAPTER 14: We Ought to Stay Together

So far, this book has focused on the point-of-view of the initiator of the divorce and partners who mutually agree to split. Now, let's look through the eyes of a partner or both partners who want to make the relationship work.

Perhaps, you and your partner can start with an inventory of what you still have together and the issues preventing you from being together — look at the good, the bad, and the ugly. Do you have any of the following feelings left in stock?

Love. While not in love anymore, there's still love, respect, and companionship left.

Partners for life. Needing a break doesn't necessarily mean a permanent breakup. Six months or a year apart in a lifetime together is a relatively small time period to reset, refresh, and restart a relationship. Ongoing separate vacations or times apart, could be solutions.

Investment. History is a valuable and rare treasure to share and it's difficult to start building with someone new.

Financial health. Freedom 75 just doesn't have the same ring to it as Freedom 55, does it?

What are your obstacles to staying together?

Fear. Fear that the behaviour that caused you to split up in the first place will continue.

Jealousy. Worry and envy that your partner is already with someone else or soon will be.

Anger. A feeling of loss of control over the situation, like when a betrayal occurred.

Exercise 12. Ready to Leave vs. Staying

It's time to balance the pros and cons for leaving vs. staying with your partner. This exercise can be helpful when you make your ultimate relationship goal, whether to make up or breakup. A counsellor or another trusted third-party can help make this kind of discussion be a productive one, as addressed in the following section.

Couples' Counseling Option

I met with Dr. Tim Clark, Registered Psychologist, in his oasis-like office, from the wicker furniture to the potted palms and low lights.

Dr. Clark said the main benefit of seeing a counsellor is to, "Get another voice in the conversation." He used the example of the retired husband who feels he's been nagged and withdraws to his workshop to escape. His solution becomes a problem for the wife, who feels shut out. They avoid having a difficult conversation. They are trapped in this pattern without that trained ear to help them get to the depths of their feelings.

Counsellors who are available through work benefits are often assigned to you at a clinic of your employer's choosing, so unless you pay for a counselor privately you don't get a choice of where to go. Even so a counsellor that you're matched up with can help come up with different perspectives and solutions.

My experience with a couples' counsellor before was mixed. Ace and I got some benefit from it; however, it had an impersonal cookie cutter feel to it.

There were a set number of sessions with homework assignments after each one. The sessions felt rushed.

The counsellor mostly took Ace's side, which made him motivated to go to the sessions. I didn't think it was all that professional of the counsellor.

She wanted to see me separately, but I declined. Certainly, it was our option to ask for a different counsellor, but we seemed to be back on track, and it was a huge inconvenience for both of us to get to these sessions. This was before virtual therapy was available like it is now.

I asked Dr. Clark what to look for in a couples' counsellor? He said to look for someone who:

- Has at least a decade of counselling experience.

- Is trained in Gottman and/or Johnson, Emotional Focused Therapy (EFT) schools of thought, which have more chance of success than other approaches.

- Will meet with you in person — not just on the phone, although, with the pandemic practitioners of all kinds switched to phone and video calls out of necessity.

- Stays neutral throughout and doesn't side with one of you. It's natural to try to get the counsellor on your side, but you want someone you're both comfortable with.

- Asks whether you want to stay together or split.

I felt more informed about the process of choosing a counsellor. However, not every couple needs a counselor to come up with a solution, as you'll see in the next story about Kari.

.

CHAPTER 15: Kari's Story: Sail Away

Kari and her partner, Chris, followed a dream many of us would envy, one filled with adventure and bliss.

While the rest of the world struggled in a pandemic, I see pictures on social media of Kari and Chris smiling on their boat sailing smoothly through this century's biggest crisis. Here's how they did it:

Kari and Chris were together for nearly a decade when they felt they were beginning to drift apart. Petite, red-headed Kari spent her free time at women's protests and consciousness-raising meetings. Tall, curly-haired and husky Chris spent his time in the pub because of her absence. They decided they needed to find a shared interest that would hold their marriage together, or it would be over for them.

They took sailing classes at the nearby marina. They talked to people who made sailing their lifestyle and were intrigued. From the beginning they loved it and made plans to do a test sail for a year. They each took a leave of absence from their jobs, rented out their house to save money, and sailed to Mexico and back. They loved the experience so much that they put their careers on hold and made a five-year plan to go sailing,

Five years went by, ten years, then fifteen, and now over twenty years later, they live on Vancouver Island in the summers and return to the warm seas of the Caribbean in the winter.

During the pandemic in 2020, they were unable to return to Canada and happily kept sailing through the turmoil the rest of the world experienced.

For some couples, the thought of living squeezed in together in the close quarters of a sailboat or an RV would be a claustrophobic nightmare, that would surely bring their relationship to a quick end.

Kari explained that in the tight quarters of a sailboat you have to work out your issues. They avoid conflict by having a clear division of chores on the boat. She takes care of the engine room and he cooks and shops for the provisions of land. They must rely on each other to overcome storms, boredom, pirates, technical problems, liquor shortages, and whatever challenges come at them on the big blue.

To finance their lifestyle, Kari said that once you stop buying stuff, you can live on an almost zero income. They sold their house in West Vancouver, bought a cheaper house and invested the difference, eventually downsizing to the condo on Vancouver Island that they rent out until they're ready to become part-time land-lubbers.

It's not all rainbows and rum, as there are real perils on the sea. Whenever a boat approaches them, Kari hides in a cupboard below deck. Chris manages whoever comes close to them on his own to protect his wife from potential rapists. They've had their boat stripped of everything a couple of times when it was in dock. Some couples may have given up by now facing these kinds of hardships. Some partners may have abandoned ship and left the other one in a foreign port to fend for themselves, but they work together as an unbreakable team.

Post-pandemic couples returned to their normal routine and decompressed, though some may spend a substantial chunk of time away from each other in a healthy temporary solution after so much togetherness. Perhaps, this might evolve into a more permanent arrangement as some couples have found they can stay together yet not live together, a practice called Living Apart Together (LAT), as described in the next section.

Living Apart Together (LAT) Couples

This solution and others that follow in this chapter are for advanced couples in long term relationships, unless you're a new couple who plans to each keep your own home. You probably want to take these up with a counsellor first before trying it. Gathered from mature couples, they are presented merely as some solutions that worked for them and allowed them to stay together happily.

When I told people that I'd left Ace, most of them were shocked. They didn't understand that he left me first in every other way but physically under our own roof.

More and more couples over 50 are finding a way to stay in their relationships by becoming LAT couples and maybe that's something that could work for us, like this couple in their 60s: Janet Billon (69) and Larry Thomas (67), described in Krishnan's article, *Living Apart, Together,* are inseparable. Except that they live in separate houses in the same gated community in West Kelowna, BC, and take long trips together, sometimes for months at a time. But asked if they plan to move in together, their response is a resounding, "No." They consider their relationship to be ideal, because they can retreat to their own homes. They don't have anything to argue about. In 2011, Statistics Canada reported about 1.9 million Canadians over 20 had a LAT arrangement.

Historically, there's a precedent for LAT, or intersecting, or parallel marriage. As Dr. Clark points out, "In the 18th century, husbands and wives had their own bedrooms. Couples became friends after the kids were raised. There was some wiggle room." The advantages of this LAT arrangement are many, including:

If the couple has adult children from previous marriages, it preserves inheritance arrangements. This avoids resentment and conflict from the adult children towards a new partner, regarding inheritances.

If they're polar opposites as far as house-keeping or habits goes, like one partner is tidy and one is a hoarder, then there's no reason to argue.

They can maintain separate finances without arguments, if one is a spender and one is thrifty, or if they just have different priorities when it comes to finances.

There is privacy and space for each partner and no arguing over the TV remote.

If one is a social butterfly and one is a hermit, then the entertainer can have friends over, and the recluse can have their peace.

Dr. Clark recommends having a contract and structure for the arrangement, or it can make couples grow further apart. For example, agree upon when you will come together and what the rules are. You may agree to have dinner together every night and, "Knock on the door before coming in."

Living apart can be a temporary arrangement with an agreed-upon end-date, where you re-evaluate the arrangement with an end to moving back in together, like six months of the year one of you lives abroad and six months of the year you live together.

There are many versions of dual households, from living next door to each other, to a tiny home in the back of the same property, to living apart in different countries for half the year. This may not be financially feasible for every couple as a marital solution. However, there are other options, depending on budget and opportunities to give each other some breathing rooms, such as:

Separate vacations.

Renting a room.

House sitting.

Staying with family or friends.

Attending retreats.

Healing Separation.

James lent me a book on healing separation. He flipped to the last page where a contract was, "See, this is what Chelsea wanted me to sign," he said. I browsed through his bookshelves and took a few others to research from his large collection of relationship books.

Piedimonte's book, a *Healing Separation,* offers an alternative to trial separations that 75% of the time end up in divorce. According to Fisher and Alberti in their book, *Rebuilding When Your Relationship Ends*, the couple signs an agreement committing to work on the relationship and the terms of the separation, usually done under the guidance of a counsellor trained in this work. At the end of the separation they can decide whether they will:

Continue the separation, like renewing a library book.

End the relationship.

Revamp their relationship.

Instead of the couple separating and concentrating on starting a new single life, this alternative has them attempt to work on their relationship while they live in separate homes without starting new relationships outside the marriage. This approach requires both partners to be willing to participate wholly in the process.

Monogam-ish

I was curious to know how millennials dealt with difficult relationships. There are many ways to restructure a monogamous relationship to include a third, fourth or more parties. An open marriage, formerly called "an arrangement," can take many forms, including:

- **Hall Pass** - As popularized in the movie *Hall Pass,* where a partner gives their partner free reign to have a one-time affair. This could be one-time permission to engage in sex with another partner, or an on-going hall pass.

- **Polyamory** - One or more partners are added to the marriage; for example, you may have one other person who shares your bed or even your home, such as in the series *You, Me & Her,* where a married couple dates a woman then she moves into their home.

This triad or "throuple" may be discrete or they may decide to be "out" about the relationship.

- **Swinging or the Lifestyle** – Swingers engage in sex with other couples, either with one other couple switching up partners or with more than one other couple. However, switching up partners without your partner present is typically off limits.

These solutions involving other parties may not be for you and your partner, especially when you're not in a solid place in your relationship. The pitfalls of these arrangements are multiple, especially since they can evoke jealousy, put you and your partner at risk for contracting STDs, conceiving an unwanted pregnancy, or experiencing harm. However, instead of going your separate ways, if both of you are comfortable exploring these alternatives, then easing into these options on an experimental, temporary or even permanent basis could be a new beginning for your relationship.

Establishing ground rules about physical and emotional intimacy with your partner is customary before embarking on an open marriage. The ground rules vary from couple to couple and may evolve. Honest communication is essential in establishing and maintaining the rules. Perhaps, a couples' counsellor can help you create and navigate your ground rules.

Trial Retirement
The last year that Ace worked, he worked a four-day week at the office in the city and one day per week at the home on the Coast where I lived. Working part-time for a year prior to retirement to ease into can be a great option,

if that's available to you or your spouse to work out the kinks in your plans.

A gradual adjustment from the 9-5 grind can provide a smoother transition. It will allow you and your partner to see how much time together is just right. It also gives you time to cultivate hobbies and social activities both together and separately, as well as get used to a new routine.

Some stay-at-home or WFH spouses, or spouses who retire before their partners, return to the office or do volunteer work when their partners retire to give each other space.

Grieving the Relationship

If your partner isn't open to reconciliation, or if you've both tried to make things work but divorce is the best solution, then it's important to recognize that you will grieve the relationship. Dr. Clark says of the grief when a relationship ends, "You don't get to not grieve. Don't distract yourself through business, alcohol, sex, food. You have to sit there with your book and your candle and go through it."

By the time I moved out the majority of my grief work was done. I was no longer sad like I was for a year of wondering if this was going to be what the rest of my life would be like if I stayed with my husband.

In the next chapter, we will look at what happens to the grandparent's rights to visitation when a couple splits. Unfortunately, in the majority of the world grandparents have no automatic authority to visit their grandchildren if their children divorce.

CHAPTER 16: You Raise Me Up
Grandparents' Rights

When couples over 50 separate or divorce, they can get comfort from being with their grandchildren, especially if their adult children have conflicting feelings about the breakup of their parents.

But not all grandparents have access to their grandchildren, because the adult children may resent the parental split, or they're going through their own separation or divorce. There are multiple reasons why their adult child denies them access.

Grandparents usually have no legal visitation rights with their grandchildren when their adult child lives with their partner in an intact relationship, and neither do they have these rights when their adult child is separated or divorced.

If their access rights are denied, they usually have to go through the courts, where a judge determines what's in the best interest of the child.

Some provinces, territories or states have statutes that specifically address visitation (access) rights for grandparents. In those that don't specifically mention grandparents, they may still petition for access just like any other interested party.

Indeed, breakups can leave grandparents in a precarious position.

In Canada, the *Divorce Act* gives courts the right to decide matters of custody and visitation, that may include the minor children's grandparents, if it's in the best interest of the children.

Key Advice:

Grandparents and great-grandparents are encouraged to ask their adult children for permission to see their grandchild, or great-grandchild before turning to a lawyer or the courts to apply for visitation orders.

Various jurisdictions have different approaches. For example, in Canada, the province of British Columbia's courts rant visitation rights to grandparents and mediation can be employed to shorten this process. In neighbouring Alberta, grandparents must first prove loss of contact with them is detrimental to the child.

It's best to check out what's available in your own jurisdiction. The Author's website has charts with click-able blue links to access specific grandparent rights resource in Canadian provinces and territories. Similar listings and click-able links are also provided for US states; the UK; Australia and New Zealand. Visit:

breakupmakeuporshakeup.wordpress.com.

Coming up next, is Sonia's story. She's a grandmother who was cut off from her grandchildren and the joy and comfort they would've brought to her life, but not because of divorce as you'll read in the next story.

CHAPTER 17: Sonia's Story: Blue
A Memoir for My Grandchildren

Sonia wrote a memoir to connect with her grandchildren in the future, because she can't see them in the present.

Her son's family is intact, so she has no legal recourse to see her grandchildren, because the children weren't being abused or neglected.

Instead, she must wait until they are grown to give them the memoir, so they will know her story and part of their family history. (If you like this idea but aren't a writer, you can make a video or audio recording for your grandchildren. You can also reach out to your local writers' association and they will help you connect with writers who can help you put together your memoir).

Sonia is an incredible resilient woman who still undertakes big projects into her senior years.

Cupid has been unkind to her, but she refuses to give up on love and life. She proudly shows me her book *Your Grandma's Story* that she wrote for her grandchildren who are kept from her by her estranged son and daughter-in-law. She hopes that one day the grandchildren will get to read about their heritage.

Sonia met her first husband, Raymond, in 1970 at her office.

She writes: "He was gentle, nice, and caring. Right then, I knew! A few days later, Raymond was waiting for me outside work. Our first outing together was playing tennis; our first kiss was at a horse race. If his horse would win, he would kiss me; his horse won, so he did."

The couple married in the summer of 1971. They settled in La Beauce, Quebec, then moved to the Sunshine Coast of BC in 1977 with their two young boys.

Sonia got a job working as a typesetter, but the hours of exacting work at the light table affected her vision. She was diagnosed with Severe Central Serous Retinopathy. She describes the terror of this condition, "Any amount of stress in my life would cause the blood vessels in my eyes to break and my vision would become impaired. Many times, my vision blurred in both eyes making it impossible to drive or to function. What worries me to this day is the accumulation of scars and permanent damage — will I become blind?"

Instead of working with her eyes, she found a job at the pulp mill doing taxing labour done by men. "I became in charge of the washers. The washers were four floors of old equipment. I was told that I was the first female washer operator since the Second World War. It was smelly, steamy, hot, noisy, dangerous, old, dirty, and unpredictable!"

Both she and Raymond worked at the mill. The exhaustion of working long hours in a physically demanding job, as well as doing most of the work building a home for her family, put a strain on the marriage and they separated. She recalls this time of quiet sadness:

The separation was sad but fairly peaceful. I sat with the boys and let them choose to stay with Raymond or to come with me. They both said that if I would leave them behind, they would walk across Canada to join me.

As soon as we arrived at my parent's house, I realized that I had made a bad mistake. We would not get any support from them. The rest of the family lived further away and were busy with their own lives. We struggled for a while, looking for an apartment, for work, for schools.

Raymond and I started talking on the phone. We could not help but express our feelings for each other. It didn't take long for Raymond to ask me if we could all come back to BC. I said yes!! Raymond was ecstatic on the phone, crying and laughing at the same time.

The family didn't have long to celebrate their reunion. Their eldest son was killed a month later in a car accident. To help her cope with the overwhelming grief, Sonia took a nurse's aide course. After eight months she got a job working with elderly people at a home. She poured her energy into her job. "I loved working with older people and taking care of them." Sonia and Raymond felt "closer than ever", but their happiness was short-lived.

At 2:00 a.m. I woke up. Raymond was agitated and trying to get up, but he fell to the floor. I turned on the light and ran to his side. Raymond was trying to stand but could not do it. At first, I thought he was dreaming, but I soon realized that this was serious. I called 911. Our place was out of town and difficult to find. It took three calls before the ambulance arrived and took him to St. Mary's

Hospital. From there they transferred him immediately to Vancouver General Hospital by helicopter.

At VGH, we waited in a small room to see the Doctor. He told me that Raymond had a brain aneurysm and was brain dead. Because he was still on life support, they needed my permission to remove support. Reality hit me and I crumbled.

Raymond was gone at only 47 years-old. Soon afterwards, Sonia she was advised not to work anymore because she had gone blind in her left eye.

Sonia's grieving spirits were lifted when a granddaughter was on the way. She moved into a condo and gave her son and his family her spacious house. A second granddaughter came along.

It was at her condo complex that a neighbour, Paul, developed an interest in her.

Paul was tall and slim and nicely groomed. He had a responsible job as a Technician engineer. After just a few dates, I was already getting concerned about his drinking, but I thought it was nervousness or shyness. As time went by, he was still drinking heavily and watching a lot of TV.

Sonia ignored the inner voice that was warning her about his drinking. The couple married in September 2002.

Soon I found out that he was financially unstable; not only did he have no money, but he had lots of debt! His condominium was bought recently with a borrowed down payment, his old car was not paid for, and his credit card was full! Not good! I was disappointed but hopeful.

Sonia built a bed and breakfast on a view property. She did all the hard work building, while Paul drank and became increasingly jealous of her.

Life with Paul was getting intolerable, and my health was getting worse. The blood vessels in my eyes were breaking again. I was getting depressed and going to bed in tears just about every night.

We decided to see a counsellor together. After a few sessions, he did not want to return. He was refusing to acknowledge that he had a drinking problem. I went to Alcoholics Anonymous meetings to see if I could help him but realized that I could not help someone that did not want to be helped. I finally told Paul I wanted a divorce.

It took me less than a few weeks to sell the house.

Newly divorced, Sonia threw herself into building another house. She reconnected with an old friend, Doug, who was a widower. She writes of their rekindled friendship:

Later that week, we decided to meet for coffee. Doug is calm, nice, nine years older than me, and similar to Raymond. I think we both needed someone nice in our lives. We felt comfortable together. Doug started to come two or three times a week to help with the house construction. It was the beginning of a new relationship, but I was worried about getting too close and getting hurt again.

However, that was five years ago, and Sonia's romantic relationship with Doug has changed. He lives in the basement of the home she moved into two years ago and they're status is good friends, rather than in a relationship.

She is comfortable with herself and would rather live on her own. She is slow to trust, saying that when you like someone at first you don't know what they're really like.

Sonia is happy with her many activities and friends, including the ones she made while raising her family and working at the pulp mill 40 years ago.

She copes with her vision loss admirably.

Among her many sorrows in life the greatest is the rift that developed with her son and his wife. Sonia is confused as to why the crevasse opened up in the first place. Her son and his family moved away, and they don't want any contact with her. Not being able to see her grandchildren is a constant ache.

Sonia could have gone to court to try to get visitation rights but would likely have lost. The memoir filled with photos captures everything in her heart that she wants her grandchildren to know about their departed grandfather, uncle, their own father's childhood, their extended family, as well as their grandmother.

Sonia sums up the lessons she learned from her life experiences:

I learned to protect myself emotionally and financially. Emotionally, I learned to love myself first and I value my own space and time. It's important for me that my creativity and friendships are not hindered by the person I cohabit with. I learned that love isn't limited to a relationship. Friends that create a safe place to bloom and grow are a big part of love. I am not sure if I will be in another relationship, but for now I am happy and at peace.

Financially, I learned that you should have a cohabitation agreement. You will be more independent and have some security for your future that way. You want to keep what you have if the relationship fails. I would like a relationship where we share the same interests. As you get older, you need someone to do things with and to care for each other.

Sonia has much wisdom to pass along from her tumultuous relationships both romantic and family, but now she is in a good place to be on her own.

Yes, it would've been an easier journey with the support of her son and continuing to be involved with her grandchildren's lives.

However, at the time of this writing her eldest grandchild has reached adulthood, so she can reach out at any time to share the long memoir that will spark conversation.

In the next chapter, I have some tips to pass along about how to thrive on your own. Not everyone will have family and friends around them during their separation and divorce. You may have moved to a new community, like I did, or you may have gone through this process during the pandemic when we were all in self-quarantine.

Maybe your friends and family aren't onboard with your choices, not all of mine were. You can do this on your own and much of this needs to be done by and for yourself.

You got this.

CHAPTER 18: Separation Hacks

I realized that my year of separation didn't have to feel like a year in limbo.

Aside from all the logistical and secretarial tasks, I wanted to set some goals and have some fun.

As the initiator of the separation, the onus was on me to do much of the work and that seemed fair.

I want to share some of the information I gathered during that time to streamline things for you.

Administrative Hacks

To make sure I didn't miss any essential tasks during my separation, I created a list of everything that had to be done as far as administration.

I agree you have to "sit with your candle and book" and grieve the end of the relationship, like Dr. Clark says, but I had this list of to-dos for when I got restless:

Make:

A monthly budget of expenses.

Change:

Surname, if you wish to, by reverting to your maiden name (women) or choosing a new name (regardless of gender). This involves a form (doesn't everything?), a fee, and publication in a local newspaper of your intent to change your name. You may want to change the name of your minor children as well.

Going back to your surname before marriage can be empowering, or even taking a new name. In her memoir, *Wild: From Lost to Found on the Pacific Crest Trail*, Cheryl Strayed describes how after her divorce, she changed her surname to "Strayed" because she had affairs outside her marriage. "I *had* strayed and that I was a *stray* and that from the wild places my straying had brought me." Not everyone would be so bold as Strayed, but she shows how you can choose an entirely new name for yourself to stake out a new life.

Change:

Mailing address to be redirected with postal service or skip the fee and send out emails and postcards to your friends, families, employers, unions, and others.

Identification as required, for example:

Driver's license.

Medical insurance cards.

Government ID, like passports.

Contact info on other cards, for example:

Rewards and loyalty cards, such as store cards, gas cards, and Air Miles;

Membership cards such as library, art gallery, and movie theatre — or get new ones.

Mailing address and contact information for government agencies, using online forms, such as:

Revenue Canada, Canada Pension Plan, Old Age Pension Plan.

Contact information for websites.

<u>Cancel:</u>

Credit cards in both names and apply for new credit card(s).

Subscriptions to services held in both names, and to your former address.

Magazine and newspaper subscriptions.

<u>Make Appointment With:</u>

Banker to cancel bank accounts in both names, open new bank accounts – order new cheques with your new surname (if applicable). Change beneficiary for Registered Retirement Plans.

Financial Advisor to see what changes you may need to make to investments (if applicable).

Human Resources (if applicable) to change beneficiary for benefits, like your pension plan, health benefits, life insurance.

Lawyer to change beneficiary of Will, Power of Attorney (PoA) and Advanced Health Care Directive (AHCD) (if applicable). Otherwise, if you're incapacitated or die, the previous instructions stand.

Trustee (if applicable), for example, for a child with special needs who needs to have or already has a trust.

Estate planner (if applicable).

Insurance agent (if applicable) to change Life Insurance policy beneficiary.

Accountant (if applicable) to see what the tax implications will be because of your separated status.

GP to discuss sexual health, get screened for STDs, including HIV if you don't know what your HIV status is, if your partner has cheated on you. For men, if you have Erectile Dysfunction get a physical to rule out any physical or other problems that may be causing it, such as high blood pressure or diabetes.

Call:

Health agency to report reduced income to get deductibles reduced (if applicable). For example, BC Fair Pharmacare reduces your deductible on prescription medications if your income drops by 20%.

Friends who are sympathetic to meet up or just chat.

Shop for:

Self-care items, like candles, soft towels, essential oils, bubble-bath, music, cosmetics, self-help books, herbal teas, scent, lotion, or anything that makes you feel pampered. Condoms, dental dams, lube, lingerie, new date wardrobe, and sex toys whether or not you're dating. You can do so online in the privacy of your home.

Consider:

Getting a pet (if your living situation allows for one). Seriously, a pet is a wonderful companion.

Living out a life-long dream, like learning to tap dance, fly, or live in another country.

Having a spa day at home or splurging at a real spa.

Other (make a note of anything else you'd like to do).

How to Make New Friends

When I moved back to the city I was in a different area, so I didn't have my circle of friends within walking distance.

I called the Newcomers' Club for that area to connect with other women new to the area. This organization is affiliated with the Welcome Wagon.

Many of the local branches are for women only, but some allow both sexes to attend. They have luncheons, coffee meetings, book clubs, game nights, pub nights, sightseeing, movie nights, wine tastings and many other activities that will keep you busy and engaged socially.

I knew about the Newcomers' Club because when Ace and I first bought a house on the Sunshine Coast we joined that branch. We met so many lovely people and were able to put down some roots.

There are lots of other ways to meet friends and singles.

Meetup.com has no or nominal fees. I met many wonderful writers and editors in several areas with the *Just Write* or *Shut Up and Write* groups. I started a similar group on the Sunshine Coast, that meets weekly

Try a Toastmasters meeting to improve your public speaking and leadership skills.

Singles clubs hold dances and other social events in most towns and cities if you're ready to mingle. Check out the events page in your local paper.

Join a running or bike club, a dragon-boat team, or beach volleyball league: https://www.active.com/

Volunteer for a charitable organization or event.

Do something unusual, like go-karting or indoor sky-diving.

Take a foodie tour of your city. Browse the farmer's markets.

Check out Eventbrite online to see what's going on near you.

Events and Adventures has activities for singles or those who've filed for divorce: www.eventsandadventures.com.

The library is a hub for clubs, such as a knitting and book clubs, writers' group, computer club, courses, talks and literary readings all for free.

If you like to sing, choirs are a fun way to connect.

If you're crafty, there are maker studios and shops that host crafters and makers, for example, every yarn shop is sure to have knit night.

Take an improv class.

Go to a paint and wine night.

Start your own group or club, like a book club, HAM radio, or other hobby club.

Take or teach a part-time course.

Start a blog.

Join or start a walking or hiking group, or a social group, like a coffee morning.

Exercise 13. My First Year of Freedom

On a separate piece of paper, jot down your social and personal goals.

Travel Hacks

People who have gone through a separation or divorce often find themselves wanting to get away to break the bond with their former partner, escape painful memories, get a change of scenery, or just do what they've never had the opportunity to do before.

If separation left you worse off financially, but you still want a change in scenery, a chance to get away and have some fun, there are ways to travel, if you don't mind mixing work with pleasure, including:

Teaching English as a Second Language (TESL) – This usually requires getting a TESL certificate that can be taken in a classroom setting or online, or some organizations train you on site. TESL instructors are in demand and can be paid well across the world. Also, you could look into teaching exchanges, if you're already a qualified teacher.

Cruise ship instructor – Work on the cruise ships as an instructor teaching a skill, such as crafts, art, dance, etc. You get a cabin onboard and time to explore the ports between your onboard classes.

Volunteering – Volunteer for programs in exotic locations — from teaching to building homes — where you live and work among local people. They can be expensive but there are probably less expensive locations and operations.

House swaps – Great for a longer-term visit in another location. Just be careful about establishing house rules.

International house-/pet-sitting – Why stop at local house-sitting jobs? If you apply for the proper visas to countries, you can house-sit and pet-sit just about anywhere you wish to experience a country.

Volunteer as a teacher in other countries - There are agencies you can go through that'll match you with an assignment and billet you with a family. Although most of these volunteer positions require that you cover your own travel and living expenses, they can be fulfilling and enriching programs.

Exercise 14.   Social and Travel Goals for my Future
It's ironic that I'm updating this in June 2020 when the border is shut and we're still social-distancing and self-quarantining.

After months of the country being shut down, I've become an expert at roasting my own coffee beans and making pour over coffee at home.

Nevertheless, I have faith that the world will open up again and we will all be able to dust off our coffee loyalty cards and passports again.

The social and travel goals I wish to achieve for myself going into the future are: (Write on a separate piece of paper or on your computer.)

Exercise 15.   Leave Vs. Stay
Pros and cons for leaving vs. staying with my partner are: (Write on a separate piece of paper or on computer.)

Exercise 16. Trying on Solutions for Size
What are some mutual goals and potential solutions to propose that you and your partner can try that might make a difference? Jot some down now—these goals can change but capture some now. (Write on a separate piece of paper or computer.)

Dating Again

At some point you may want to find a new partner, or just go on a date. Going out with someone new can be a real boost to your self-esteem, and a way to casually meet new people who may end up being friends if not romantic interests.

It's also a great way to get out of the house and enjoy healthy outdoor or cultural activities you enjoy.

To ease into dating, you might want to try something like speed dating where you go to a public place and spend just a few minutes chatting, then there's a rotation until you've met with every potential date in the room.

At the end of the event. each participant writes down who they'd like to go on a one-on-one date with.

If the participants match up, they're given a safe way to contact each other.

Online Dating 101

In Mary Vega's book, *Divorce After 50, What Now?*, there's advice for creating a "super" online dating profile:

Make it a happy and positive profile with photos of you smiling and maybe participating in any of your hobbies.

Think of a great username that describes some element of you. And follow that with an interesting headline or opening line to your profile. Make the main body of your profile concise and positive, even add some humour if you can. . . Above all be honest.

There are plenty of dating apps that my younger readers are far savvier about than I am, so I will focus on sites specifically for mature people, such as:

www.eharmony.com

www.dating.elitesingles.com

www.ourtime.com

www.seniorpeoplemeet.com

www.christianmingle.com

www.OKCupid.com – This site has a detailed questionnaire and is free. A writer friend met her mate there and a friend of hers met his wife on this site.

Plenty of Fish (https://www.pof.com) - A free site.

SEX

Unfortunately, the incidence of STDs, including HIV and AIDs is on the rise for mature adults, who are less likely to practice safer sex than younger adults.

However, this doesn't mean you have to forego sex now that you are single and over 50.

Dr. Forrest recommends the following guidelines:

Have open discussions with your health professionals about personal dating issues, your own sexual activity, and your concerns about STDs.

Read about STD transmission online or in pamphlets.

Know your HIV status. Keep copies of your test results to show to your intended partner.

Talk to potential partners about their HIV status and ask to see their STD results.

Have a supply of condoms and don't have unprotected sex.

Remember James from earlier in the book, who married a younger woman who walked away after they had a baby for another man? James' has found that as he's aged, the emotional connection with a partner is more important when it comes to sexual performance.

Not knowing if he can perform with a new partner can lead to nervousness, to the point where nothing happens when the big moment comes.

He says it can be a vicious cycle, so it's better to take the Erectile Dysfunction (ED) medication to break the cycle.

The combination of medications for ED in men and Hormone Replacement Therapy (HRT) for women are part of why the over 50s have increased incidences of STDs.

Also, according to the CPHA as we age our immune systems weaken, so we are more susceptible to infections.

CHAPTER 19: Navigating Divorce Laws

If you are concerned about your safety if your partner were to discover what's in your browser history, see the FAQ - How Do I Keep My Partner from Knowing What I've Looked at on My Browser? in the *Introduction*.

Disclaimer: Best efforts were made to find free, up-to-date and accurate forms and information related to divorce for each country. This information is subject to change. Consult legal aid, a lawyer, or do your own Internet search. Be aware that while legislation may say one thing the actual practice can be much different.

Please Note: Author's website has detailed listings, URLs and, in some cases, phone numbers, for arbitration and mediation services regarding Canadian provinces and territories, American States, the UK (England & Wales, Scotland and Northern Ireland), Australia and New Zealand. See: breakupmakeuporshakeup.wordpress.com.

Canada

Residency

You must live in the province or territory you are applying for divorce for a year before you can apply for divorce there. You must also be a Canadian resident to divorce in Canada. Unless as non-residents you got married in Canada, and the country where you both live doesn't recognize your marriage.

No-fault Divorce

Canada has a no-fault divorce law after a couple has been separated after a year, which is governed at the federal level. Each province has its own property laws and regulates separation and divorce.

Legal Separation

Canada doesn't recognize legal separation (where couples are separated but remain legally married); however, couples can create their own *Separation Agreement* as previously described in this book.

Common-law Marriage

Canada recognizes common-law marriage after couples have lived together for a specified time, for example, in Alberta it's three years and in British Columbia it's two years.

Same-sex Divorce

Canada recognizes same-sex marriage and divorce.

US

In the United States there are no federal laws governing separation and divorce, rather each state governs its own divorce laws, so you have 50 states to leave your lover to choose from. The individual states are also in charge of laws surrounding common-law relationships. This web page gives you links to all the states and their marriage, annulment, separation and divorce laws:

www.hg.org/divorce-law-basics.

Residency

It doesn't matter which state you were married in when filing for divorce, but whichever state you file for divorce in you must be a resident in the state for anywhere from 30 days to a year, for example, Kentucky, Maryland, and New Hampshire, prior to filing for divorce. The typical time of residence required is six months.

Let's say you got married in Arizona but moved to Texas, one of you has to be a resident of Texas for at least six months before filing for divorce there. All states seem to make an exception for military personnel.

No-fault Divorce

Iowa, that also recognizes same-sex marriage, has no-fault divorce. Kentucky is a no-fault divorce state with one ground for divorce, that is an "irretrievable breakdown of the marriage". Minnesota and Nebraska have this same ground for divorce as Kentucky. Arizona, Massachusetts, Michigan, New York, and Washington are also no-fault divorce states. Missouri has one ground for divorce that the marriage is "irretrievably broken" and recognizes legal separation.

Grounds for Divorce

Grounds for divorce vary from the expected to the surprising, such as if a woman is pregnant most Texas courts won't finalize the divorce until after the baby is born. Even if the baby is NOT the husband's child. Seemingly contrary as many states specify when a woman is pregnant with another man's baby it's a ground for divorce.

Many states include some of the following as grounds for divorce aside from irreconcilable differences:

Cruelty

Adultery

Committing a felony

Incarceration

Abandonment

Insanity, or being a patient in a mental hospital

Impotency

Habitual use of alcohol, cocaine, opium, morphine and similar drug

Bigamy

Attempting to kill your spouse

Not supporting your spouse financially

Alabama has biblical wording in their grounds for divorce, such as, "The commission of a crime against nature, with man or beast, either before or during marriage." New Jersey cites similarly outdated language by stating deviant sexual behaviour is a ground for divorce.

Illinois is the only state where infecting your spouse with an STD is a ground for divorce.

New Hampshire has this ground for divorce that probably isn't used often, when a spouse has "joined any religious sect… which professes to believe the relation of husband and wife unlawful".

Covenant Marriage

Arizona would be unremarkable with its no-fault divorces, except for their Covenant Marriages. Mixed-sex couples who are already married or those entering into their first marriage can choose to have a marriage for life that's more difficult to obtain a divorce from. Arkansas and Louisiana also have Covenant Marriages.

Dissolution of Marriage

California, Florida, Illinois, Minnesota, and Oregon have a streamlined process called the "dissolution of marriage" for couples with no children and a small net worth. For these couples there's no trial or hearing required.

In California, the couple has to have been married five years or less, whereas in Illinois and Minnesota the couple can be married up to eight years or less.

Oregonian couples, including those in a domestic partnership, have up to ten years to participate in the dissolution of marriage process.

Ohio and Pennsylvania have both a no-fault dissolution of marriage and a fault-based divorce.

Forced Counselling & Reconciliation

In Connecticut, a judge may require a couple to try to reconcile their differences. Idaho has similar reconciliation proceedings. Kansas, New Hampshire, and Ohio courts may order the couple to seek marriage counselling. See this link for divorce forms for each state: www.divorce-forms.net.

Common-law Marriage

Texas has some unique marital, common-law, and divorce laws, for example, there's no difference between a ceremonial or common-law marriage in Texas. For a common-law marriage to be valid, the couple only has to meet three criteria:

Agree that they're married.

Live together as husband and wife.

Tell others that they're married.

There's no specific time period that the couple has to wait after moving in together to be common-law married. They could live together a day and tell everyone they're married, wear wedding rings, address each other as husband and wife, thus meeting the legal requirements as long as they are of legal age (18), not related to each other, and not married to someone else. If they want to end the marriage, they must get a divorce, annulment, or wait until death they do part, just like a couple married in a church or civil ceremony.

Same-Sex Divorce

California, Maine, Nevada, New Jersey, Oregon, Washington, and Wisconsin recognize the union of same-sex couples. To end a Domestic Partnership the partners, file a *Petition of Dissolution of Domestic Partnership* with the court. In Illinois, both same-sex and mixed-sex couples can enter a Civil Union, equivalent to a marriage. For more information on Domestic Partnership by state, visit www.hg.org/divorce-law-domestic-partnership

UK / England & Wales

England and Wales have no-fault divorce and legal separation for married or same-sex couples in a civil partnership. You must be married for at least one year before applying for divorce. For more information, you can go to the following link:

www.gov.uk/separation-divorce.

The UK remains under EU divorce proceedings law, despite the Brexit vote at the time of this writing. If you and/or your spouse live in England or Wales for at least a year prior to applying for divorce, you meet the rules for habitually resident. However, rules of habitually resident and domiciled are complex. Visit this site for more information if an overseas divorce applies to your case: www.gov.uk/government/publications/overseas-divorces

Common-law Marriage

Common-law marriage doesn't have validity in the UK, except in Scotland where some basic laws exist if the couple breaks up. Couples who live together need to have a *Cohabitation Agreement* to set out the terms of property, support, debts, inheritances and other details if they want to share these responsibilities and privileges: www.lawdonut.co.uk/personal/divorce-and-family-law

Same-Sex Divorce

Same-sex couples are united in a legal civil partnership, as well as mixed-sex couples who don't want the religious connotations of traditional marriage. If they want to end the partnership, they go through a dissolution, which is the same process and outcome as a divorce.

Scotland

In Scotland, you must be married at least a year before you can get a divorce. You can get a legal separation.

There are five grounds for divorce, as follows:

Adultery.

Unreasonable behaviour.

Desertion for two years.

Lived apart for two years and both agree to the divorce.

Lived apart for five years - it doesn't matter if your partner doesn't agree to the divorce.

For more information on separation and divorce in Scotland, you can go to this link:

https://www.citizensadvice.org.uk/family/ending-a-relationship/how-to-separate/ways-to-end-your-marriage/

Northern Ireland

In Northern Ireland, you can't get a divorce or a dissolution of a civil partnership for same-sex partners until you've been married or in a civil partnership for two years. After the two-year period, the grounds for divorce are the same five as in Scotland. There are four possible reasons for dissolution for a civil partnership:

Separation for 2 years with the consent of the other partner to dissolve the partnership.

Separation for 5 years.

Unreasonable behaviour.

Desertion.

For more information on separation and divorce in Northern Ireland, you can go to this link:

www.nidirect.gov.uk/articles/getting-divorce-or-dissolving-civil-partnership. Also, go to:

www.gov.uk/divorce for a step-by-step online guide.

Australia

Australia has a no-fault divorce law. For more information and a Do-It-Yourself kit, visit this link: www.familycourt.gov.au

Residency

You can file for divorce in Australia if you usually live in Australia and were living in Australia for a year before filing for divorce.

Common-law Marriage

Common-law marriage is not a term used in Australia, at least not to describe an unwed couple who lives together, instead the term *de facto* marriage is used after a mixed-sex or same-sex couple has lived together for two years. *De facto* marriages can be registered.

Same-Sex Divorce

Same-sex couples who have had their relationship solemnized are treated the same as other married couples when it comes to divorce. Same-sex couples can register their relationship as *de facto* marriages, as can mixed-sex couples who live together. If a registered *de facto* marriage breaks down, the couple can divide their

property through the courts:
www.gotocourt.com.au/family-law/de-facto-relationships.

New Zealand

New Zealand has a no-fault "dissolution of marriage" or "civil union" law. You have to live apart from each other for two years and at least one of you must live in New Zealand permanently to apply for dissolution of marriage: (www.justice.govt.nz/family/separation-divorce).

Residency

Their rules on being "domiciled" are complex and can be seen at: https://www.justice.govt.nz/family/separation-divorce/apply-for-a-d. Go to: https://www.govt.nz/browse/family-and-whanau/separating-or-getting-divorced/how-to-get-divorced-in-nz/ for more information.

Common-law Marriage

Common-law marriage is not a term used in New Zealand to describe an unwed couple who lives together, instead the term *de facto* relationship is used. After a mixed-sex of same-sex has lived together for three years they have the same rights as a couple who are in a marriage or civil union, except they can't jointly adopt (www.justice.govt.nz/family/separation-divorce/divide-relationship-property/relationships-covered-by-law/).

Same-Sex Divorce

Same-sex marriage has been possible since 2013, so same-sex couples who marry go through the same dissolution process as mixed-sex married couples.

CHAPTER 20: Emergency, Transition & Safe Homes

As outlined earlier, there is also a degree of screening for family violence, when you're filling out a law firm intake questionnaire, so you'll need to disclose if you're afraid of your partner and reasons for your answers.

You'll also need to divulge if the police have been involved with your family in any way and details of this.

As well, you'll need to say if you're comfortable meeting with your partner in the same room and if not, state the reasons why.

You'll also need to outline any concerns you may have regarding the safety of your children, and provide any concerns you may have regarding your partner's mental and emotional health, violence and any alcohol or drug abuse concerns.

This chapter examines some disturbing statistics on the levels of violence against partners – and it also features a list of available resources n Canada, the US, the UK, Australia and New Zealand.

In Canada or the US, if you are concerned about your safety and in case of emergency, call 9-1-1, or call your community police.

You can also go through the court system to get orders to stop your partner from stalking you and causing you harm.

As well, an internet search for women's shelters will generate a list of such facilities in your community area in Canada or the US, UK, Australia or New Zealand.

If you are concerned about your safety if your partner were to discover what's in your browser history, see the FAQ - How Do I Keep My Partner From Knowing What I've Looked at on My Browser? in this book's *Introduction* for full details.

Some key points include: Keeping your browsing history private or sending emails that can't be traced back to you. The newer and better way is to use your browser's Incognito mode to do your private browsing.

Every browser has a different way of using Incognito mode, so use Google for instructions on how to use it with your browser. This is a pretty good way to stay private.

For a higher level of privacy, use a computer that isn't affiliated with you in any way, like at a library or Internet café; don't login to any of your usual email or social media apps, because as soon as you login everything else you do can be traced; at a safe computer create a new secret email and/or social media accounts and never login to them from your home or work computers; ensure there is no way to trace them back to yourself by not using any personal information. Full details are in the Introduction.

If you're in an abusive relationship, make a plan and practice how you will get out safely. If you are being abused, call the police if it's an emergency.

Canada

In Canada, intimate partner violence accounts for a quarter of all police-reported violent crimes – and two-thirds of intimate partner violence incidents are at the hands of a current partner, according to Statistics Canada.

Spousal homicide is also highest after separation. Canadian women are six times more likely to by killed by their spouse following separation than prior to separation, although non-fatal common assault accounts for the majority of violence incidents.

In case of emergency, **call 9-1-1**, or call your community police. You can also go through the court system to get orders to stop your partner from stalking you and causing you harm. Go to www.sheltersafe.ca and find your province and www.bwss.org. For full links go to the book website at: breakupmakeuporshakeup.wordpress.com.

Please note that violence against women – particularly by intimate partners – is a problem in most countries throughout the world, including our study group of featured nations of Canada, the US, the UK and Australia and New Zealand.

The national number to call in emergencies is 9-1-1 t o be put in touch with police and other services.

A welcoming atmosphere is also provided by Newcomers' Clubs. The national club website is at www.nnac.ca for a complete list of such resolurces, go to the Author's book website at:

breakupmakeuporshakeup.wordpress.com.

US

In the US, in case of emergency, **call 9-1-1**. This link has advice on what to do legally about domestic violence: www.hg.org/legal-articles/dealing-with-domestic-violence

You can also go through the court system to get orders to stop your partner from stalking and causing you harm. Go to www.domesticshelters.org and look up your state for shelter information. Links are provided at the book website at breakupmakeuporshakeup.wordpress.com.

Violence against women is a disproportionately huge problem in the United States where women are 11 times more likely to be killed with guns that women in other high-income countries such as Canada, UK, Australia and New Zealand.

In fact, female intimate partners in the US are more likely to be killed with a firearm than all other means combined.

The presence of guns throughout the US increases the risk of homicide for women by 500% and more than half of the women killed by gun violence die at the hands of family members or intimate partners.

Indeed, intimate partner violence in the United States is a major problem, affecting more than 12 million Americans every year. According to the National Domestic Violence Hotline (1-800-799-7233). On average, more than one in three women and one in four men will experience rape, physical violence and-or stalking by an intimate partner.

As well, one in 10 high-school students has experienced physical violence from a partner in the last year alone. Statistics like these demand that we all commit ourselves to ending abuse for good.

An average of 24 people per minute are victims of rape, physical violence or stalking by an intimate partner in the United States — more than 12 million women and men over the course of a single year.

Just under 15% of women (14.8%) and 4% of men in the US have been injured as a result of intimate partner violence that included rape, physical violence, and/or stalking by an intimate partner.

Almost half of all women and men in the US have experienced psychological aggression by an intimate partner in their lifetime (48.4% and 48.8%, respectively).

Four out of five victims of intimate partner violence or women – and women ages 18 to 34 and 25 to 34 generally experience the highest rates of intimate partner violence.

More disturbing US stats: Nearly one in five women have been raped in their lifetime – about half of them were raped by an intimate partner, and most of these victims also sustained injuries or symptoms of post-traumatic stress disorder.

Nearly one in three college women (29%) report being in an abusive dating relationship – and a third of women killed in US workplaces die at the hands of current or former intimate partners.

Although women are more likely to become victims of stalking (one in six women) and other forms of abuse, it's worth noting that one in 19 men also experience stalking or other forms of abuse, most often by current or former intimate partners.

In households with children where spousal violence is a problem, 22% of these children witnessed violent incidents and in 30-60% of such households, the children themselves are also abused. – and studies have shown children in these situations are 15 times more likely to be physically and/or sexually assaulted than the national average.

UK & Wales

Call 9-9-9 if it's an emergency. Contact your local policing team if it's not an emergency. The following organizations can give you help and advice about domestic abuse.

Freephone National Domestic Abuse Helpline, run by Refuge - 0808 200 0247 www.nationaldahelpline.org.uk

Galop (for lesbian, gay, bisexual and transgender people) - 0800 999 5428 www.galop.org.uk

Live Fear Free helpline (Wales) - 0808 80 10 800 www.livefearfree.gov.wales

Men's Advice Line - 0808 801 0327 www.mensadviceline.org.uk

Rape Crisis (England and Wales) - 0808 802 9999 www.rapecrisis.org.uk

Respect phoneline - 0808 802 4040 www.respectphoneline.org.uk

Scotland

Scotland's Domestic Abuse and Forced Marriage Helpline - 0800 027 1234 sdafmh.org.uk

Scottish Women's Aid - 0131 226 6606 www.scottishwomensaid.org.uk

Northern Ireland

Women's Aid Federation - 0800 917 1414
www.womensaidni.org

Australia

In case of emergency, **call 0-0-0.** For more information, go to this link:
http://www.familycourt.gov.au/wps/wcm/connect/fcoaweb/family-law-matters/family-violence/

Family Relationship Centres - Call 1800 050 321 or visit Family Relationships Online:
https://www.familyrelationships.gov.au/

1800 RESPECT - 1800 737 732

www.1800respect.org.au / 24/7 Crisis line: 1800 737 732

www.familyviolencelaw.gov.au

Mens line - 1300 789 978

National Domestic Violence Counselling Service 1800 200 526

Australian Capital Territory: Domestic Violence Crisis Service (24 Hours) - (02) 6280 0900

New South Wales: Domestic Violence Line - 1800 656 463

Northern Territory: Darwin Sexual Assault Referral Centre (24 Hours) - (08) 8951 5884

Darwin Domestic Violence Counselling Service - (08) 8945-6200   / Lifeline Top-end - 131 114

Alice Springs – Women's Shelter - (08) 8952 6075

Queensland: Brisbane Domestic Violence Advocacy Service - (07) 3217 2544 / D V Connect - 1800 811 811

Women's Legal Service Smartphone App: Re-Focus: https://www.wlsq.org.au/resources/legal-toolkit/re-focus-app/

South Australia: Domestic Violence Crisis Service (24 Hours) - 1300 782 200

Domestic Violence Helpline (24 Hours) - 1800 800 098

Tasmania:

Family Violence Referral Line (24 Hours) - 1800 633 937

Victoria:

Magistrates' Court of Victoria - Family Violence: https://familyviolence.courts.vic.gov.au/

Women's Crisis Service Victoria: 1800 015 188

The Men's Referral service: 1800 065 973

Western Australia: Women's DV Helpline (24 Hours) - (08) 9223 1188 or 1800 007 339

Men's DV Helpline (24 Hours) - (08) 9223 1199 or 1800 000 599

Victoria Legal Aid - Family violence video

New Zealand ; If you're in immediate danger, **dial 111** or **105** and ask for the police, or go to your local police station.

For more information on how to get help if you're in an abusive relationship, go to: https://www.justice.govt.nz/family/family-violence

For help finding shelter go to: ttps://womensrefuge.org.nz

Family Court

0800 224 733 - justice.govt.nz/family/about

Find a Lawyer: lawsociety.org.nz

Free Legal Advice: communitylaw.org.nz

Legal Aid: justice.govt.nz/courts/going-to-court/legal-aid/

Shelter

Women's Refuge: 0800 733 843 - womensrefuge.org.nz

Help Lines:

Are You OK: 0800 456 450 - areyouok.org.nz

Shine: 0508 744 633 - 2shine.org.nz

Shakti: 0800 742 584 - shakti-international.org/shakti-nz/

Safe to Talk: 0800 044 334 - safetotalk.nz

Victims Information: 0800 650 654 - victimsinfo.govt.nz

sexualviolence.victimsinfo.govt.nz

Citizens Advice Bureau

0800 367 222 – cab.org.nz

Family Services Directory

familyservices.govt.nz/directory

For full links go to the Author's book website at:
breakupmakeuporshakeup.wordpress.com.

Adieu – Best Wishes for Your Journey

As I mentioned at the beginning of this book, I'm not a relationship guru, legal genius, or financial wizard. I'm just a person who went over a big bump in the road with their partner of over 35 years — a bump called retirement. I had to figure all of this out on my own, so I wanted to share it with you to make your breakup or make up or shake up less ominous.

Exercise 17. Trying on Solutions for Size

You've read the stories of many people who have been through a separation, divorce, or a reconciliation. Reflect on those stories and choose which one(s) most resemble your relationship and why. (Write on a separate piece of paper oron your computer.) Express what you've learned from their stories Use the heading: This is MY Story – and write down your own experiences and responses.

I wish the best for my readers and contributors as your journey unfolds. It's my hope that the stories and resources shared in this book help you on your shining new path.

Bibliography – Research References:

Abeykoon, H. & Lucyk, K. (2016, January 26). Sex and Seniors: A Perspective. *CPHA Policy & Advocacy Blog*.

Adcox, S. (2017, February 3). Grandparents' Visitation Rights in Canada. *The Spruce*:.

--. (2019, September 17). Grandparent Visitation Rights by State. *VeryWell Famiy.*

Anderson, K. M.S. & MacSkimming, R. (2007). *On Your Own Again: The down-to-earth guide to getting through a divorce or separation and getting on with your life.* Toronto, Ontario: McLelland & Stewart, Inc.

Atwood, M. (1986). *The Handmaid's Tale.* Toronto, Ontario: McClelland and Stewart Inc.

Australian Government. (2017.) *Divorce Rates in Australia.* Australian Institute of Family Studies.

Blackmon, M. (April 16, 2020). *Coronavirus is Pushing People to Revisit Relationships that Fell Apart.* Buzzfeed News.

British Columbia Ministry of Attorney General. (2017). Who Can Help? *Family Justice.*

Boyd, JP. (2017, June 27). *JP Boyd on Family Law.* John Paul Boyd and Courthouse Libraries BC.

Bunpar. (2013). *Divorce After 50: 50 Things to Do with Your Life After a Gray Divorce Over 50.*

CBC. (2013, March 19). Family Law Act Says Common-Law Couples Are Considered Spouses After Two Years. *CBC News.*

Centre for Public Legal Education Alberta. (No Date*). Grandparents' Rights.*

Clark, T. (2017, June 22). Interview with Dr. Tim Clark. North Vancouver, BC. Canada.

Cole, D. (2015, January 19). Forget "Gray Divorce": Here's How to Make Love Last. *The Wall Street Journal.*

Covy, K. (2016, April 27) *Tips for surviving divorce after 50.*

(2017, August 24). 50 Shades of Grey Divorce. *Huffington Post.*

Connor, K. (April 3, 2020) "Curbing COVID-19 may lead to increased divorce rates." *Toronto Sun.*

Curry, H., Clifford, D. & Hertz, F. (March 2002). *A Legal Guide for Lesbian & Gay Couples* (11th Ed.) Berkeley, California: Nolo.com

Dennis, W. (2016, June 3). How Grey Divorce Became the New Normal. *Everything Zoomer.* Zoomermedia Interactive Network.

Devine, M. (2014, February 10). The Five Stages of Grief and Other Lies that Don't Help Anyone. *Huffington Post.*

Draaisma, M. (2010, July 20*).* Sexual infections on the rise among Middle-Aged Canadians. *CBC News.*

Dreger, A. (2013, February 1). *When Taking Multiple Husbands Makes Sense.*

Dubé, Dan-ielle, (2017, June 16) *Should you get a prenup or cohabitation agreement before settling down?* Global News.

Enright, M. (2017, January 27). 'Til grey do us part: the dramatic rise of grey divorce. (Excerpt from Ashley Walter's documentary *The High Dive)* CBC Radio, *Sunday Edition.*

Fies, A. (April 17, 2020) S*urge in divorces anticipated in wake of COVID-19 quarantine.* ABC News.

Fisher, B. (No Date). *The Healing Separation: Agreement Form.* Noeticus Counseling Center. Denver, CO.

Fisher, B. (No date). *The Healing Separation: An Alternative to Divorce or Ending.* Denver, Colorado: Noeticus Counseling Center and Training Institute.

Fisher, B. & Alberti, R. (2005). *Rebuilding When Your Relationship Ends, Third Edition.* Atascadero, California: Impact Publishers, US.

Forrest, D. A. (2017). Dating and sexual activity in Canadians over 50: a pioneering frontier. *More than Words: The Official Blog of the British Columbia Psychological Association.*

Gold, B. (2017). *Gray Divorce Stories: The Truth About Getting Divorced Over 50 From Men and Women Who've Done it.* DivorcedOver50.com.

Gold, K. (2016, April 4). Chinatown development has Vancouverites worried about neighbourhood's future. *The Globe & Mail.*

Gottlieb, L. (May 18, 2020). Dear Therapist: My Boyfriend Had an Affair Now We're Stuck at Home Together. *The Atlantic.*

Government of Canada. (1999). *Transition Houses and Shelters for Abused Women in Canada.* Health Canada.

(May 15, 2020). *COVID-19: Managing financial health in challenging times.* Financial Consumer Agency of Canada.

Graveland, B. (April 19, 2020). *Baby boom to breakups: Here's how COVID-19 is testing relationships.* The Canadian Press.

Halt.org. (N/d.) *The Process of Moving on a Comprehensive Guide to Divorce in Canada.*

Hasseldal, K. (April 20, 2020). *More divorces after COVID-19? California attorney says 'Absolutely'.* CBS8.

Hendrix, H. & Hunt, H. L. (2013). *Making Marriage Simple: Ten Relationship-Saving Truths.* New York , New York: Harmony Books.

Johnson, C.C. (1984). The Retired Husband Syndrome. *The Western Journal of Medicine*, *141*(4), pp. 542-545.

Johnson, S. (2008). *Hold Me Tight: Seven Conversations for a Lifetime of Love.* New York, New York: Little, Brown and Company.

Kelly, M. (2007). *The Seven Levels of Intimacy: The Art of Loving and the Joy of Being Loved.* New York, New York: Simon and Schuster.

Kirshenbaum, M. (1997). *Too Bad to Stay, Too Good to Leave*. New York, New York: Penguin Group.

Krishnan, M. (2012, December 16). For Better or Divorce. *North Shore News.*

Krishnan, M. (2013, September 17). Living Apart, Together. *Maclean's.*

Lesser, E. (2005). *Broken Open: How Difficult Times Can Help Us Grow.* New York, New York: Random House.

McLeod, S. (2007, updated 2016). *Maslow's Hierarchy of Needs.*

McCombs, B. (2016, September 12, 2016). 'Sister Wives' appeal polygamy ruling to U.S. Supreme Court. *The Salt Lake Tribune*.

Marlo, J.D. (2012, April 2,). *How to Survive Grey Divorce: What You Need to Know About Divorce After 50.* California, US: Van Law Offices of Marlo Van Oorschot, JD.

Maveal, A. (2017, May 29.) What is sologamy and why are women doing it? *Global News*.

Mitnick, K. (2017, February 14). *The Art of Invisibility: The World's Most Famous Hacker Teaches You How to Be Safe in the Age of Big Brother and Big Data.*

Moddasser, H. (2017). *Gray Divorce, Silver Linings: A Woman's Guide to Divorce After 50: Field Guide Series Book 1.* Chapel Hill and Greensboro, North Carolina: Stearns Financial Group.

O'Hare, J. (2016). *Through the Dragon's Gate: Memoirs of a Hong Kong Childhood.* Gloucestershire, UK: Mereo Books. UK.

Neustaeter, B. (June 15, 2020). *Living with an Ex: When Pandemic Breakups Don't Mean Separating.* CTV News.

Newman, S. (April 3, 2020) More Babies or More Divorces After COVID-19? How disasters do, or don't, affect fertility and divorce. *Psychology Today*.

Office for National Statistics. (2014.) Marriage and divorce on the rise at 65 and over.

Park, V. (2017, April 26). Personal Communication. Vancouver, BC, Canada.

(2017, June 30). Personal Communication. Vancouver, BC, Canada.

Patel, (2020, April 27). *Minister says COVID-19 is empowering domestic violence abusers as rates rise in parts of Canada.*

Pawlitza, L.H. (n/d) "Can I Get Divorced During the COVID-19 Pandemic and Other Burning Law Questions." *The Financial Post*.

Penney, A. (1982, April 15). *How to Make Love to a Man.* New York, New York: Dell Publishing.

Pickford, J. (2019, September 16). Divorce Dividing Up the Family Home. *Financial Times*.

Piedimonte, J. (2016). *When Gray Divorce Strikes.* Joe Piedimonte: Self-published.

Rowan, J. (2015, June 7). Divorce Rate Up for Older Couples. *New Zealand Herald* Sawyer, A. (2015). *British Columbia Do Your Own Divorce Kit,* (2nd. Ed.) North Vancouver, BC: Self-Counsel Press.

Sawyer, A. (2008). *If You Love Me, Put It in Writing.* North Vancouver, BC: Self-Counsel Press.

Sheehys, G. (1974). *Passages: Predictable Crises of Adult Life.* New York, New York: The Penguin Group.

Sonia. (2014). *Your Grandma's Story.* Sonia: Self-published.

Strayed, C. (2013). *Wild: From Lost to Found on the Pacific Crest Trail.* New York, New York: Vintage Books.

Taub, (April 14, 2020). *A New Covid-19 Crisis: Domestic Abuse Rises Worldwide.* New York Times.

Vega, M. (2017). *Divorce after 50. WHAT NOW?* Mary Vega: Self-published.

Viorst, J. (1986). *Necessary Losses: The Loves, Illusions, Dependencies and Impossible Expectations That All of us Have to Give Up in Order to Grow.* New York, New York: Fireside, US.

USA Today. (2013, November 14,). Beware the Retired Husband Syndrome. *Thestar.com.*

Weiner-Davis, M. (2008, March 30). The Walkaway Wife Syndrome. *Psychology Today.*

Weyman, S. (July 12, 2016). 11 Signs Your Financial Advisor Is Robbing You Blind (And How To Stop It!). *How to Save Money.*

Williams, S. (2019, November 8). *Divorce-led property sales on the rise amid recent downturn, experts say.*

Wilton, A. C. & Semple, N. & Macdonald & Partners LLP. (2015). *Spousal Support in Canada (3rd. Ed.).* Toronto, ON: Carswell.

Wray, M. (April 6, 2020). *China's divorce rates rise as couples emerge from coronavirus quarantine.* Global News.

Yoshido-Butryn, C. (April 16, 2020) *Will self-isolating lead to more divorces? A family lawyer weighs in.* CTV News.

Manor House
905-648-4797
www.manor-house-publishing.com